Soviet Breakout

Brassey's Titles of Related Interest

Related Journals

[Specimen copies available on request]

ARMED FORCES JOURNAL

DEFENSE ANALYSIS

Soviet Breakout

Strategies to Meet It

JOSEPH CHURBA

PERGAMON-BRASSEY'S
International Defense Publishers, Inc.

Washington New York London Oxford Moscow
Beijing Frankfurt São Paulo Sydney Tokyo Toronto

U.S.A. (Editorial)	Pergamon-Brassey's International Defense Publishers, 8000 Westpark Drive, Fourth Floor, McLean, Virginia 22102, U.S.A.
(Orders)	Pergamon Press, Maxwell House, Fairview Park, Elmsford, New York 10523, U.S.A.
U.K. (Editorial)	Brassey's Defence Publishers, 24 Gray's Inn Road, London WC1X 8HR
(Orders)	Brassey's Defence Publishers, Headington Hill Hall, Oxford OX3 0BW, England
PEOPLE'S REPUBLIC OF CHINA	Pergamon Press, Room 4037, Qianmen Hotel, Beijing, People's Republic of China
FEDERAL REPUBLIC OF GERMANY	Pergamon Press, Hammerweg 6, D-6242 Kronberg, Federal Republic of Germany
BRAZIL	Pergamon Editora, Rua Eça de Queiros, 346, CEP 04011, Paraiso, São Paulo, Brazil
AUSTRALIA	Pergamon-Brassey's Defence Publishers, P.O. Box 544, Potts Point, N.S.W. 2011, Australia
JAPAN	Pergamon Press, 8th Floor, Matsuoka Central Building, 1-7-1 Nishishinjuku, Shinjuku-ku, Tokyo 160, Japan
CANADA	Pergamon Press Canada, Suite No. 271, 253 College Street, Toronto, Ontario, Canada M5T 1R5

Copyright © 1988   Pergamon-Brassey's International Defense
Publishers, Inc.

First edition 1988

Library of Congress Cataloging-in-Publication Data

Churba, Joseph.
   Soviet breakout.

   Includes index.
      1. Soviet Union--Foreign relations--1975-
2. World politics--1985-1995. 3. Soviet Union--
Foreign relations--United States. 4. United States--
Foreign relations--Soviet Union. I. Title.
DK289.C48   1988   327.47   88-12538
ISBN 0-08-035981-7

Contents

Acknowledgments

My thanks are due to colleagues in the International Security Council, including the many gifted scholars, strategists, and statesmen convened under its auspices. Indeed, in the privileged capacity as ISC President, I have benefited greatly from more than thirty international seminars, discussions, briefings, and publications focused on the Soviet threat. Given this wider setting, I am grateful for the inspiration, challenging ideas, and intellectual support so necessary for a work of this kind. I have had the advantage of extensive discussions with Eugene V. Rostow, Charles M. Lichenstein, and William R. Van Cleave. Their suggestions were highly valued. Aaron D. Rosenbaum has been a most helpful research associate. Fortunately, our friendship did not stand in the way of his precise criticism and fine editorial hand. However, in fairness to my associates, I alone remain responsible for the facts, interpretations, or inadequacies herein.

About the Author

Formerly senior policy adviser to the U.S. Arms Control and Disarmament Agency, Joseph Churba is president of the International Security Council and editor in chief of the journal *Global Affairs*. A graduate of Brooklyn College and the National War College, with a Ph.D. in international relations from Columbia, Dr. Churba once served as senior Middle East intelligence estimator for the Air Force and as professor of Middle East studies at the Air University. His publications include *The Politics of Defeat: America's Decline in the Middle East* (1977), *Retreat from Freedom* (1980), and *The American Retreat: The Reagan Foreign and Defense Policy* (1984). Dr. Churba's lecture tours take him around the world, and he appears frequently on radio and television.

The author is pleased to dedicate this work to the Reverend Sun Myung Moon in recognition of his lifelong struggle for peace and freedom.

CHAPTER 1

Introduction

At the time this book was written, the drama of the Iran-Contra affair was still unfolding. At first glance, this dismal episode appeared to have little to do with the larger questions of the Soviet threat and America's response to it, but in fact, the relevance was direct. This book deals with strategy, and the Iran-Contra affair represented an unalloyed failure of both strategy and tactics. As such, it illustrates many of the institutional and intellectual problems that afflict the United States in its confrontation with the Soviet Union, a strategically deft and disciplined power.

RESOUNDING BLUNDER

Let us consider for a moment the strategic and tactical failures implicit in the Iran-Contra initiative. First, the Reagan administration went ahead with the decision to engage Iran without any clear, long-term objectives, save the generalized hope for better relations and the desire to promote regional stability. Despite claims to the contrary, the administration seems to have spent little time considering how the Iranian revolution might have *permanently* changed the regional balance, the psychological outlook among regional governments, the regional image of the United States, and the nation of Iran itself. Practically no attention was paid to how the success or failure of the Iran initiative as then conceived might affect such long-term considerations as the growth of Islamic fundamentalism, stability and perceptions of stability in the Persian Gulf, and Iran's continuing politico-psychological relationship with a nation it regards as the "Great Satan."

Second, the United States did not assess what Iran's own strategy

1

might be: whether the appearance of a division within the ruling group might be a trap, what things aside from hostages Iran was prepared to give to the United States, and what tactics the Iranians were likely to employ given past experience and current practice. The United States failed to apprehend Iran's cultural viewpoint, deciding instead to assess the Gulf, the war with Iraq, and Iran's relations with the United States through an American prism. Nor did the United States articulate and understand Iran's agenda, even though the Iranians by both deed and action had demonstrated that they did not necessarily embrace the pragmatism of Western policymakers and their concomitant "common sense."

Third, and in part because so much of the operation was conducted in self-conscious yet porous secrecy, the operatives of the initiative toward Iran did not build a series of scenarios, nor did they test them theoretically or with limited exposure "laboratory exercises." The United States became locked into a single-track strategy that quickly degenerated into a no-strategy, limited-tactics gambit. This permitted the Iranians to readily assess the limits and intentions of America's plans.

Fourth, American policymakers relied too much upon self-interested Iranian, Israeli, and American middlemen for the strategic assessment upon which the American initiative was based. Operatives at the National Security Council (NSC) and the Central Intelligence Agency (CIA) did not believe or recognize sufficiently that the middlemen might have different priorities or simply different bases of perception that would render their guidance inappropriate.

Moreover, the responsible American policymakers apparently did not consider that even if the information provided by Manucher Ghorbanifar, Amiram Nir, Richard V. Secord, and others were sound, they approached the matter as businessmen: they viewed the entire matter as one more deal, to be determined mainly by tactics, without any reference to larger or long-term implications. And since they were used to making exchanges of credit for commodities, the degeneration of the deal into a simple swap of arms for hostages did not trigger in them the same sense of alarm that it would in a policymaker attuned to other costs, not just financial ones.

Fifth, there was little thought given to how various powers within the Iranian leadership might be reinforced, both positively and negatively, by calculated American actions. Having posited the existence of a potentially friendly, pragmatic moderate group, the United States gave that group no real reason to make its fortunes within the Iranian leadership contingent upon satisfying America's desires or, at minimum, not embarrassing the United States. Analogously, the United States did not communicate to its adversaries in the Iranian leadership, directly or indirectly, what costs they would incur if they derailed America's opening to Iran and, in so doing, damaged America's interests. Little attention was paid to the sort of mischief that opponents within the Iranian leadership might cause and how the effect might be minimized. Neither did the United States consider the prospect of treachery from its erstwhile moderate clients. Instead, having almost arbitrarily identified certain individuals as "moderates," the United States hoped against hope that they could deliver all that the United States wanted and that the extent of their dealings with the "Great Satan" would not be discovered.

Sixth, the United States offered various military and diplomatic emoluments to the Iranian leadership without informing the Iranians of any associated cost of refusing them. Similarly, these concessions were offered in a disconnected, piecemeal fashion, with no regard for how the relationship between the two governments could be made more secure and more civilized, step by step, with each projected exchange. The United States did not address the psychological dimension of the conflict, nor did it demand that the Iranians show evidence of their moderation in concrete terms acceptable to the United States. Thus, the United States allowed itself to be forced into playing the game on Iran's tactical terms and diminished any chance that the Iranians would be coaxed or forced into a relationship congruent with America's expectations and standards.

The Iranians were able to retain their cultural disposition of viewing the United States as a mortal enemy. The United States did not find a way to deny to the Iranians (or have the Iranians deny to themselves) the utility of America-bashing as a political weapon. Thus when the deal was exposed, even the speaker of the Majlis, Hashemi Rafsanjani, assumed to have an interest in better relations with the United States, felt free to attack and ridicule the United States openly. The scope of the defeat thus included the *tactical* failure of not gaining freedom for the hostages, with the *political* failures still being felt in region, and the *psychological*—yet strategic in nature—failure of not advancing Iran's internal dialectic about its relationship with the United States.

Seventh, the United States did not evaluate seriously the potential regional and international effect that the collapse of this initiative might have. No consideration of worst-case scenarios was made, despite claims to the contrary, nor was any time spent considering how a measure of success might be extracted from a collapsing situation. Thus, when the U.S.-Iranian diplomacy was exposed, the United States was able to salvage nothing. Such absolute disasters simply are not that common in world politics, even though the United States has suffered them repeatedly in recent years and has come to accept them as a survivable, even acceptable outcome.

Eighth, before the final collapse of the deal, when the larger ambition of a normalized relationship evaporated, the United States abandoned any strategic notions for the short term, purely tactical objective of gaining the freedom of the hostages. Yet even this was pursued in a manner that experience had already demonstrated would not elicit an acceptable Iranian response. Indeed, the very decision to pursue it convinced the Iranians that they could chisel the United States even further and without incurring any cost. Here, too, the purely tactical approach was implemented without sufficient consideration of the quality of the intelligence behind the decisions that had been made. Nor was enough consideration paid to the possible impact the discovery of a simple arms-for-hostages deal might have upon America's larger interests, including the desire for regional stability, America's leadership of the free world and the war against international terrorism.

Ninth, even in this small, hopefully low-key tactical game, the United States failed to evaluate how its gambits and tactical objectives might be foiled by such simple things as leaks to the press, the changing of conditions previously understood to have been resolved, and the seizing of more hostages. Indeed, even as hostages such as the Reverend Benjamin Weir were being released in exchange for weapon shipments, other hostages, their value as a currency now established, were being seized in Lebanon at the behest of the Iranian leaders. The failure of the United States to dissuade the Iranians from this behavior, or even reprove them for it, was especially counterproductive. Worse, the serial release of individual hostages even as more hostages were being seized was greeted in the National Security Council with jubilation. The Iranians probably anticipated this reaction; it reinforced the American desire to continue with the already fatally compromised initiative, and it reinforced the Iranian desire to exploit American naïveté for all it might be worth.

Tenth, throughout the entire process, there was no serious independent effort made to assess and challenge the intellectual and political foundation of the operation. The group in charge of the Iran-Contra effort never confronted a Team B from within the NSC, the CIA, or elsewhere. Moreover, because some of its activities were either illegal or in contravention of established practice, secrecy became a matter of self-protection, and the interests of the United States were made hostage to the desire of the planners of the Iran-Contra affair to prevent exposure.

In retrospect, it seems hard to believe that so pathetically incompetent an operation as this was allowed to go forward, especially with so much American credibility riding on it. The Iranian leadership, by refusing to trade all the hostages, by sanctioning the murder of CIA Beirut station chief William Buckley, by seizing more hostages, by exposing the entire operation, and by evincing no concern about reprisal—demonstrated how much it was a master of its own strategy and how contemptuous it was of America's amateurism.

Equally disconcerting was the assumption within the Reagan administration that the losses incurred here were transient and of little long-term value, when in fact this nation is only beginning to discover how much of its international standing has been squandered by this adventure. No less disturbing were the institutional suggestions that America's abiding economic strength and leadership of the Free World would mean by default that the United States would pay no real penalty for having tried and failed so miserably in the Iran-hostage deal.

There was an almost juvenile attitude in the administration's response, a mixture of unjustified bravado and shirking of responsibility, combined with a willing disregard for any long-term costs. It seemed as if the United States had arrived at an era of diplomacy-as-arcade-game. In contrast, Iran had followed the dictum of the Ayatollah Khomeini: "Nothing in life is funny. Everything is deadly serious."

A MORE FORMIDABLE OPPONENT

Reviewing the Iran-Contra affair is particularly instructive because it represents *in extremis* precisely the sort of things that can and do go wrong with America's strategic and tactical approaches to ideologically committed nations that obey an integrated strategic vision hostile to our interests. The Soviet Union is the textbook example of such an opponent. Much more than in our dealings with Iran, U.S.-Soviet relations comprise an area in which the very survival of the nation and the Free World is at issue. Moreover, this is an area in which the United States confronts a resourceful opponent, culturally distinct from us: innately aggressive; mindful of its own weaknesses; willing to make the most of its strengths; committed to well-defined, long-term objectives; and capable of exercising a surprising degree of tactical flexibility and strategic patience. All of America's international diplomacy requires consistency and control. In particular, its dealings with the USSR—both directly and on behalf of allies, clients, and economic interests—must be reflect a cohesive world view, a unified strategic vision, and tactical discipline to a much greater degree than any of the rest of our diplomacy.

Unfortunately, this has rarely been the case. The United States has used and continues to use its considerable economic strength and the enormous appeal of freedom and democracy to counteract Soviet salients in both central and peripheral arenas.   Yet the Soviet Union has not scaled back, let alone abandoned, its aggressive designs, and the assumption that the appeal of the American model alone will forever prove sufficient to best Soviet expansionism seems intellectually naïve and politically dangerous.   As with our adventure with Iran, it puts too much at stake, while relying on an ill-considered counterstrategy based on the kindness of strangers. These actions do not become a superpower and cannot effectively meet the wide-ranging ambitions of Soviet expansionism.

CHAPTER 2

Soviet Culture, Soviet Threat

Before embarking on this analysis and the concomitant prescription, we should consider a fundamental question: how real is the Soviet threat? Too often, East-West relations are defined by strategic arms control negotiations. Yet precisely because such talks comprise a dialectic, the implication is that both sides are equally responsible for world tensions and that the grievances of both sides are equally deserving of redress. One well-established reason the Soviet Union engages in arms control talks is to protect its own material advantages while diminishing those of the West. Yet it can be argued that the primary reason the Kremlin engages in such "statesmanlike" pursuits is to gain a cloak of legitimacy for its foreign policy as a whole. By normal standards, little of Soviet foreign policy, aggressive and adventuristic as it is, would merit such legitimacy.

Western policymakers, often dazzled by the image of statesmanship, have played into a larger Soviet strategy by embracing arms control and the entire culture of arms control. This, in turn, has created the situation where Western politicians and diplomats, mindful of the political investments they have made on behalf of arms control, become interlocutors on behalf of Soviet behavior. One consequence of this dialogue is self-censorship or, even worse, the suspension of critical faculties, which in normal circumstances would characterize Soviet foreign policy for what it is. Thus, policymakers fail to educate Western voters about the endemic and systemic nature of Soviet and Russian expansionism.

There is indeed a Soviet threat, and its nature is fundamentally, qualitatively different from any American threat that might be posed against the USSR. It is this difference that explains why the implicit premises of arms control—that the superpowers are more or less equally to blame for world tensions and that both engage in the process for

7

essentially the same reasons—are profoundly wrong.

Soviet political objectives are formulated within the context of an ideological framework structured on the belief in the inevitability of change. The Soviet leadership views itself as carrying out its historic responsibility by setting the pace and direction of change in the world's social and political environment. By contrast, to the limited extent that U.S. political objectives are enunciated at all, they are rarely formulated within the context of a comprehensive world view, but rather in reaction to events precipitated for the most part by others. The predominant tendency in U.S. political aims is toward preservation or restoration of the status quo. The U.S. focus is thus on maintaining the balance of power, while the Soviets are irreversibly committed to continually changing the "correlation of forces" in their favor.

While the Soviet Union seeks to exploit every opportunity to hasten the demise of the system of free, autonomous, and pluralistic societies, the United States and its allies have confined themselves to attempting to parry the challenges to their very survival. Any advocate of the status quo, however, is at an inherent disadvantage when he is no longer in a position to wield overwhelming countervailing force against an opponent determined to pursue the course of revolutionary change.

Political objectives intended only to maintain or to restore the status quo are anachronisms in a world where the fundamental premises underlying the very concept of politics and international political relations as understood in the West are rejected by the Soviets as being out of touch with the dynamic realities of the historical process. The Soviet leadership is convinced and acts on the premise of its ultimate victory in the struggle for global hegemony, while the U.S. maximum articulated objective has been the containment of Soviet expansionism, a reactive goal of striving to maintain the status quo.

While the policy of containment can claim success to date in preventing Western Europe, Greece, and Turkey from succumbing to Soviet overlordship, it has had little effect in restraining Soviet expansionism in Asia, Africa, and Latin America. One need but glance at a world map showing the extent of Soviet control and influence in 1947 when the containment policy was first put into effect, and compare it with the Soviet reach today to recognize the relative ineffectiveness of containment as a preeminent geopolitical objective. This is especially true when one considers that forty years is a brief period when judged by the standards of world history or the standards by which emerging empires are judged.

It serves little purpose to dwell on the occasional setbacks, both great and small, suffered by the Soviets as evidence that the Soviet advance is not inexorable. Losses such as those experienced in Egypt and Somalia are more than compensated for by Libya and Ethiopia, the latter having become a full-fledged Marxist-Leninist state.   The split with China, while creating significant problems for the USSR and constituting a serious thorn in its side, does not offset the very substantial gains achieved by the Soviets throughout the Third World.   The Soviets themselves are not overly disturbed by such setbacks.   Lenin taught them well that the road to revolutionary achievement would not be smooth, that they would sometimes be required to take "one [large] step forward, two [small] steps back."   Nor is any setback viewed as final. When conditions are right, renewed revolutionary thrust will overcome the obstacles in the road.

SOVIET IMPERIALISM

In his classic work, *Politics Among Nations*, Hans J. Morgenthau wrote:

> A nation whose foreign policy aims at acquiring more power than it actually has through expansion of its power beyond its frontiers, whose foreign policy, in other words, seeks a favorable change in power status, pursues a policy of imperialism.

According to Morgenthau, imperialism may thus be defined "as a policy which aims at the overthrow of the status quo, at a reversal of the power relations between two or more nations."

For more than four hundred years, under the tsars and later under its Soviet mantle, Russia has pursued an unrelenting policy of imperialism.   Russia was a relatively homogeneous nation centered in northern Europe between Finland and the Ural mountains, until the latter part of the sixteenth century, when the Russians began a drive for empire that makes other such attempts pale by comparison.   By 1700, the tsars ruled most of the northern half of the Eurasian land mass from Poland to the Pacific Ocean, all of which was incorporated into the Russian state.   By the outbreak of World War I, the empire had expanded to the south, swallowing up nations and petty states of southeastern Europe and central Asia.

The very character of the tsarist empire created conditions that effectively precluded Russia from following the course of development that saw the rise of the modern nation-states in Europe and the Americas.   While the Russians constituted a majority in the tsarist state, the empire was nonetheless comprised of many nations that could not be readily assimilated into one nation-state.   And, as with all empires in modern history, pressures began to build that promised to tear apart the multinational colossus.

The chaos that ensued as a consequence of the war, followed by revolution, encouraged a bevy of separatist national movements. Indeed, before taking power, Lenin himself recognized the right to self-determination of all peoples, even if such were to result in the dissolution of large parts of the Russian state. Separatist movements predicated on national self-determination arose in Byelorussia, Finland, Estonia, Latvia, Lithuania, the Ukraine, Armenia, Georgia, and Turkestan. However, once having succeeded to the Kremlin, Lenin and the Bolsheviks took steps to prevent the breakup of the new Soviet state. While the Treaty of Brest-Litovsk (March 3, 1918) wrested a large segment of the western portion of the empire from Soviet control as part of the price for peace, the new leadership was determined to maintain the integrity of the multinational state by a novel approach.

The ideology that Lenin made into the state religion subordinated national differences to the transnational class struggle. Class cut across the lines of nationality, and the transnational unity of the proletariat would become the organizing principle of the new Soviet empire. Thus, while Lenin was still able to proclaim the inherent right of all peoples to national self-determination, the exercise of that right was to be constrained by the higher needs of the worldwide class struggle. To facilitate the eventual victory of the proletariat, the empire was to be preserved intact, and so it was in fact. What proved effective in defense of the sphere under direct Soviet control also became the hallmark of the Soviet forays abroad into ever-widening spheres of adventure and influence.

Soviet imperialism became rampant at the end of World War II, as Soviet armies occupied all of Eastern Europe, and measured over the subsequent four decades, the Soviet threat has only increased in ferocity. The Baltic states of Estonia, Latvia and Lithuania were quickly reintegrated into the empire, while East Germany, Poland, Czechoslovakia, Hungary, Romania, and Bulgaria became vassal states or satellites. Finland was given a new and unique status that added a new word to the political lexicon, *Finlandization*.

In Asia, the Soviet Union effectively absorbed Mongolia, although it maintains nominal sovereignty, annexed southern Sakhalin and the Kurile Islands, established close linkage to the communist regimes of North Korea and Vietnam, and invaded Afghanistan. In Latin America, Cuba has long since become a Soviet dependency, while Nicaragua is on the verge of Sovietization. In addition, the Soviet Union has brought within its embrace the Marxist states of Ethiopia, South Yemen, Angola, and Mozambique, while a number of other states are candidates for entry into the Soviet sphere of influence. Throughout, the motive force and means of enforcement behind the Soviet drive for empire has remained a constant.

WHAT MAKES THE SOVIET THREAT UNIQUE?

In essence then, the Soviet threat has always been capable of being described by several fixed characteristics, which distinguish Soviet imperialism from any other such threat in the world today.   First, expansion by military means has been the hallmark of the Russian state for the last six centuries.   Imperialism has been the *normal* state of affairs for every leader in the Kremlin.   The growth of the Soviet military and the increasing role the military plays in Soviet life, combined with the high success rate demonstrated in recent years, suggest that the Soviet leadership perceives little negative cost in pursuing a long-term policy of aggression.   From the Soviet point of view, the West has done little in the last forty years to negatively reinforce the Soviet leadership from its natural propensity for military expansion.

Second, the Russian leadership and the Russian people have always viewed this expansion as evidence of their state's legitimacy.   Russian leaders have always been sole proprietors of the Russian state.   This is as true today of the Soviet *nomenklatura* as it was of the tsars.   As in centuries past, within the Russian state a class with the standing or legal power to challenge or to restrain from within the leadership's aggressive behavior does not exist.   Moreover, the leadership of the Russian state continues reflexively to view imperialism as the best means of demonstrating or reinforcing its legitimacy.

Third, the power to expand, to threaten, and to coerce are similarly taken within Russian society as evidence of the Russian state's standing and power and as a means of legitimizing the leaders of the state.

Fourth, the economics that drive Russian and Soviet aggressiveness are not those of imperial mercantilism but those of poverty.   As Richard Pipes explains in *Survival Is Not Enough*, "Poverty necessitated expansion; expansion necessitated large military outlays; and large military outlays robbed the country of productive resources, perpetuating poverty." There is nothing positive or reformist about the Soviet drive for empire, despite rhetoric to the contrary.   Even apart from the normal imperial desire for national aggrandizement, the motive behind Soviet imperialism is primarily one of control, exercised by an oligarchy fearful of those it does not control.

Fifth, the USSR now finds itself with an economy and work force increasingly unable to compete with those of the West.   Having failed to create an economy that produces finished industrial or consumer goods competitive in the world market, the USSR faces a crisis of capital starvation for its internal economic development. It can sell abroad raw materials and weapons, but these generate insufficient funds for investment and modernization. The enormous natural barriers that block the development of Soviet Asia, combined with the poor state of the Soviet infrastructure, exacerbate this situation.

Sixth, the Soviet Union, like Russia before it, aggressively legitimates its imperialism through a chauvinistic ideology that in its legalism and inflexibility borders on the religious. Russian Orthodoxy gave an unambiguous sanction to the expansion of Holy Mother Russia. Marxism-Leninism, as interpreted and trumpeted by the Kremlin, provides the same rationale today for the expansion of the Russian "workers' state."

Seventh, self-serving political validation is backed up by the threat of unmitigated violence. Satisfying Russian and Soviet claims or putative security concerns has not diminished the willingness of the Soviet leadership to employ open threats of force and subversion. On the contrary, the Russians' willingness to use such threats has only been reinforced by each imperialist success.

Eighth, the Soviet Union adheres to a long-term strategy for expansion. The Soviet leadership has demonstrated that it is willing to seize opportunities as they arise. Its behavior also confirms that it values losses for the West almost as much as gains for the Soviet Union. Consequently, the USSR readily varies its demeanor and exploits Western weaknesses and fears in order to divide and paralyze its opponents and capitalize on opportunities. It discounts criticism and is little deterred by it; neither does it give credibility to counterattacks, for experience has shown that few such ripostes to Soviet imperialism last very long. Only when the USSR stands to undermine its opponents' position does it enter into true dialogue. The Soviet state, like the Russian state before it, is incapable of true self-criticism in partnership with foreign powers, perceiving this as a sign of weakness and an implicit attack on its legitimacy.

Thus, the world confronts a nation psychologically and politically inclined toward aggression and impelled economically to either parasitize or conquer outright the economic resources it needs. These resources are essential not only for long-term development but for maintenance of the current economy and for the continued political control and legitimacy of the Soviet leadership. *This will remain so, whatever the outcome of the so-called Gorbachev reforms*.

The strategy mounted by the United States to meet the Soviet threat can only exist in this context. It is in reaction to *this* Soviet threat, not a milder or less determined one that some might posit, that the validity of America's anti-Soviet strategy, such as it is, will be tested. There will be no other battleground, nor can this battleground be avoided. A strategy that does not register viscerally on the Soviet Union as it understands itself by definition will not succeed.

Until now, a signal failure of the West has been the refusal to examine or articulate the cultural differences (both Russian and Soviet) that distinguish the threat of Soviet imperialism and to construct a policy that specifically conforms to the reality of the USSR as a Russian and Soviet state and not as a Western state in the making. Analogously, the United States has failed to educate its citizens and the people of the West about the qualitative difference in the Soviet threat. It seems possible here that the operant wisdom has been that such an effort would go over the heads of the average citizen of the West. But the popular appreciation of cultural differences is widespread; it forms, after all, the basis of most hostile propaganda against the enemy in time of war. So policymakers should not be deterred so quickly by the supposed difficulty of the task.

Polls in the summer of 1987 revealed that residents of Western Europe were as likely to credit the USSR as the United States for recent contributions to arms control; the polls also showed that both superpowers were viewed as sharing approximately equal responsibility for the state of relations. These nonsensical, potentially suicidal perceptions are likely to become ever more credible if the United States does not as the first part of its defensive strategy accurately characterize the nature of the Soviet threat. It must do so as reflexively as the Soviet Union characterizes its own motives and as often.

The Soviet Union is currently seeking a new period of détente with the West, one that will afford it the opportunity to consolidate its gains of the past decades and establish a new threshold for the next phase of its drive for world domination. Today the Soviet Union is the center of an empire reaching out from the Eurasian heartland to the farthest corners of the globe, led by a leadership that equates Soviet imperial ambitions with historic necessity. The leaders of the Free World must recognize the character of the Soviet state and its unwavering commitment to the destruction of the pluralistic system of the industrial democracies. There is nothing obscure about Soviet objectives. The USSR has made them quite clear, by its actions if not by its declarations.

Yet having talked endlessly of the disastrous nature of nuclear war, the USSR has succeeded in defining international discourse in such a manner that challenging the USSR too aggressively is viewed as a certain path to global suicide. This has given the Soviet Union a power to coerce on a global scale that formerly it did not possess. Now the

Union is seeking tactical superiority by the achievement of "escalation dominance," the perception that the USSR always will have the will and the means to respond ever more forcefully to Western salients against it or its interests. The pursuit of escalation dominance is the centerpiece of the Soviet tactical plan, and as such it is analyzed in greater detail in chapter five.

Suffice it to say here that possession of sufficient escalation dominance would give the Soviet Union de facto world domination without having to pay the military or political costs that normally would be required. Given the primacy Russian and Soviet political psychology assign to the attainment and maintenance of control, it should be evident that the Soviet Union cannot be bought off or somehow finessed out of this ultimate achievement. Only a response that makes Soviet strategy untenable holds the promise of success. Each Soviet victory—tactical or strategic; military, psychological, or political—makes the mounting of an effective counterstrategy that much more difficult. Yet even now it is not an impossible task.

The very desire on the part of the Soviet Union to enhance its position by psychologically terrorizing its adversaries about its intentions and capabilities is a central part of Russian and Soviet culture, manifested in strategy. Achieving this power to coerce is a central part of Soviet national strategy. Yet despite Soviet pretensions, the power of the USSR is not yet the sole determinant of international politics, nor need it be. But the United States cannot effectively challenge the Soviet strategy to achieve this dominance without changing the way in which the American people and the citizens of the West view the nature of the Soviet threat and the underlying motives of Soviet statements and actions.

If it fails to make its case—and it will take some years to redefine the international discourse toward this reality—then the United States will find itself fighting an endless series of indeterminate tactical battles and losing most, sapping its will to contest the USSR, even while failing to alter the Soviet psyche and thus to deter ever greater Soviet aggression.

In confronting a preternaturally aggressive Soviet Union, the United States must appreciate the long-term, dialectical nature of the conflict. It must be guided not so much by Clausewitzian approaches, which, far removed from their architect, allow tactics to be equated with strategies and battles to be equated with wars. Instead, the United States should follow the dictum of Sun Tzu, the Chinese military expert who 2,500 years ago wrote, "Thus, what is of supreme importance in war is to attack the enemy's strategy; next best is to disrupt his alliances. . . ."

Before it can be suggested how the United States should respond to the Soviet threat, it is essential to consider in greater detail the full extent of Soviet approaches to conflict. One must also assess where Soviet salients are most likely to occur, and why, so that American policy may be tailored to deter Soviet aggression while strengthening America's own interests and those of the democratic West. These concerns are the subject of the chapters that immediately follow.

CHAPTER 3

The Brezhnev Doctrine

Any political arrangement to be negotiated with the Soviet Union must be predicated on a clear understanding of the political objectives of the players. However, it is precisely in the formulation of coherent and consistent political objectives that the United States has suffered from chronic weakness, a weakness continually and successfully exploited by the Soviets to their advantage and to the detriment of the Free World.

In contrast, parallel to the most recent wave of Soviet expansionism, the Kremlin has evolved a theory of empire that in its full articulation as the Brezhnev Doctrine poses a frontal challenge to the very foundations of international law and the relations between states. The Brezhnev Doctrine represents the most self-validating aspect of Soviet strategy, the full fruition of Soviet policy by intimidation. The implications of this pernicious doctrine must be kept clearly in mind, for the Brezhnev Doctrine illustrates—in profoundly cultural and political terms —how truly dangerous are the aims of Soviet imperialism.

EVOLUTION IN SOCIALISM

The Brezhnev Doctrine was not concocted out of whole cloth in 1968. It is the culmination of a doctrinal development that reaches back to the early years of the Soviet Union, beginning with the concept of "proletarian internationalism." In 1920, at the Second World Congress of the Communist International (Comintern), Lenin defined proletarian internationalism as requiring that the interests of the class struggle in any individual country be subordinated to the broader interests of the international proletariat and the defeat of capitalism. The Communist Party of the Soviet Union (CPSU) was presumed to provide the leadership of the world communist movement in setting the needs and goals of proletariat internationalism. A resolution of the Fifth World Congress in 1925 declared that the experiences of the CPSU, "insofar as they had international significance," could be mandated for the different communist parties as necessary.

In 1943, Stalin abolished the Comintern for tactical reasons and promulgated the theory of "different roads to socialism." This in effect permitted the communist parties, which were under Moscow's control through the Comintern, to cooperate with nationalist elements in their countries in the common national interest. This tactic ultimately contributed significantly to the communist seizure of power and the establishment of "people's democracies" in Eastern Europe and Asia in the wake of the Allied victory in World War II.

To some extent, Stalin's tactic backfired when Tito in Yugoslavia and Mao Zedong in China took the theory of "different roads to socialism" seriously and rebelled against Moscow's authority to dictate policy to them. Chastened by the loss of control over Yugoslavia and China, Stalin made the theory inoperative and moved to assert Soviet hegemony over the people's democracies in Eastern Europe on the basis of a reborn doctrine of "proletarian internationalism," which was given renewed prominence. The Soviet empire no longer sought to incorporate the East European countries directly into the USSR. Stalin's new strategy was to secure his geopolitical objectives by controlling a ring of vassal states, nominally sovereign but subject to the requirements of "proletarian internationalism," as a buffer region to provide strategic depth for the USSR and forward deployment for Soviet power projection.

Stalin's iron grip on the satellite nations proved very costly. His successors sought to reestablish control on the basis of cooperation rather than coercion and reintroduced the theory of "different roads to socialism," which was given formal sanction by the CPSU at its Twentieth Party Congress in February 1956. However, in his commentary on the "different roads" theory, chief party theoretician Mikhail Suslov offered an interpretation of the theory within the context of "proletarian internationalism" that was to prove of critical importance in the years ahead. As stated by Boris Meissner in his monograph *The Brezhnev Doctrine*, Suslov maintained that

> the transition to a communist system of rule is irreversible, independent of the forms and methods used. All attempts at restoration of the overthrown class of exploiters are to be opposed with organized resistance.

REBELLION

Hungary

The implications of this principle were tangibly demonstrated later that same year when in October, the Soviets were confronted for the first time by the prospect of the defection of a country from the "socialist community." On October 22, Hungarian students set forth a sixteen-point program for reform in the communist state that included, most notably, withdrawal of the Soviet troops stationed in the country in accordance with the Warsaw Pact of 1955, a multiparty political system, and free elections. Over the next few weeks, this act precipitated a series of events that culminated in direct Soviet intervention to prevent the collapse of the communist regime. On October 30, the Soviets issued a statement dealing with the relationships between the USSR and its communist allies that in part was intended to send a signal to the Hungarians that reversion to a non-Marxist-Leninist system was unacceptable. The statement read, in part:

> The defense of the socialist gains of People's Democratic Hungary is today the chief and sacred obligation of the workers, peasants and intellectuals, of all Hungarian working people. The Soviet Government expresses confidence that the peoples of the socialist countries will not allow external and reactionary forces to shake the foundations of the people's democratic system, won and reinforced by the selfless struggle and labour of the workers, peasants and intellectuals of each country.

The intent of the message was apparently misunderstood, if not deliberately ignored, by the Hungarian leadership. On the same day, the government of Imre Nagy withdrew from the Warsaw Pact and terminated the single-party status of the Communist party. The Kremlin decided to intervene. To provide a facade of legitimacy for its obvious violation of Hungary's sovereignty, the Soviets helped János Kádár establish a new Hungarian Communist Party the very next day and a new government by November 4. Kádár promptly requested Soviet aid in putting down the revolution and in ousting the Nagy regime, aid that the USSR was only too pleased to extend to a fraternal state. This provided the desired fig leaf to cover the direct Soviet intervention, which had begun on October 31, five days earlier.

As noted by Nicholas Rostow in his study "Law and Use of Force by States: the Brezhnev Doctrine," the USSR

> emerged from the Hungarian crisis with a mature theory of the law governing international use of force. A Soviet sphere of influence in Eastern Europe had existed since 1945. Now Moscow had proclaimed and applied the rules by which that sphere was defined and governed. The Soviet Communist Party was *primus inter pares* and

the Soviet Union could use force to regulate its relations with other communist states and to keep communist governments in power.

During the dozen years that followed the Hungarian affair, the Soviets became deeply involved in ideological warfare with the two communist states that had managed to elude Stalin's grasp, Yugoslavia and China. Although the Chinese were strongly supportive of Soviet intervention in Hungary, they, aided by Tito, zealously sought to undercut the determinative role sought by the Russians in the communist world. As a consequence of this internecine ideological strife, the Kremlin found it inexpedient to press the matter of Soviet hegemony. However, it was not long before a new crisis in the Soviet empire once again forced the Kremlin to make clear that, while the sovereign right of secession from the socialist community might theoretically belong to the satellite states, "proletarian internationalism" would not as a rule permit the exercise of that right.

Czechoslovakia

The military intervention by the Soviet Union and its satellites in Czechoslovakia on August 21, 1968, marked a major turning point in the Soviet drive for global hegemony. The immediate issue was the emerging reform movement in Czechoslovakia that, as its leader Alexander Dubcek put it, was to result in "socialism with a human face." Czechoslovakia's reform movement was applauded by the leaders of both Yugoslavia and Romania, who saw it as reinforcing their own deviations from Moscow's orthodox communism. The Soviet leadership, however, saw this development as a challenge to Soviet hegemony in Eastern Europe and as a weakening of the essential unity of the socialist universe under Soviet leadership.

On July 3 of that year, Leonid Brezhnev declared ominously that the Soviet Union could never be indifferent to "the fate of socialist construction in other countries, to the common cause of socialism and communism in the world." On July 15, the Soviet Union, in conjunction with Poland, Hungary, Bulgaria, and the German Democratic Republic— the states that were shortly to intervene in Czechoslovakia—issued the "Warsaw Letter," addressed to the leadership in Prague, that saw developments in Czechoslovakia as a danger to the "common life interests" of other socialist countries. The letter went on to state:

> We cannot assent to hostile forces pushing your country off the path of socialism and creating the threat that Czechoslovakia may break away from the socialist commonwealth. This is no longer your affair alone. It is the common affair of all Communist and Workers' Parties and states that are united by alliance, cooperation and friendship.

It is the common affair of our countries, which have united in the Warsaw Pact to safeguard their independence, peace, and security in Europe to place an insurmountable barrier in front of the schemes of imperialist forces, aggression and revanche. . . .

The frontiers of the Socialist world have shifted to the center of Europe, to the Elbe and the Bohemian Forest. And never will we consent to allow these historic gains of socialism and independence and security of all our peoples to be jeopardized. Never will we consent to allow imperialism, by peaceful or nonpeaceful means, from within or without, to make a breach in the socialist system and change the balance of power in Europe in its favor. . . .

Our countries are bound to one another by treaties and agreements. These important mutual commitments of states and peoples are founded on a common desire to defend socialism and safeguard the collective security of the socialist countries. Our parties and peoples are entrusted with the historical responsibility of seeing that the revolutionary gains achieved are not forfeited.

Each of our parties bears a responsibility not only to its own working class and its own people but also to the international working class and the world Communist movement and cannot evade the obligations deriving from this. Therefore we must have solidarity and unity in defense of the gains of socialism, our security and the international positions of the entire socialist commonwealth.

This is why we believe that it is not only your task but ours too to deal a resolute rebuff to the anticommunist forces and to wage a resolute struggle for the preservation of the socialist system in Czechoslovakia.

Again, as in the case of Hungary in 1956, Moscow's message was not clearly understood. The Czechs apparently felt secure in pursuing their internal reforms. Also, there were significant differences between what was taking place in Prague and in Budapest. The Czechs were not advocating or planning the overthrow of single-party rule by the communists, nor did they intend to withdraw from the Warsaw Pact. What they thought they were doing was pursuing a different road to socialism, a course that was supposed to be acceptable within the socialist community and compatible with the prevailing interpretations of the constraints of proletarian internationalism.

Moscow's message became clear on August 21, with the invasion of Czechoslovakia by Soviet troops and small contingents from four Warsaw Pact allies: East Germany, Hungary, Poland, and Bulgaria.

Subsequent to the intervention, which clearly violated not only the rules of international law but also the principles of socialist international law, Soviet ideologists evolved a theory of "limited sovereignty" and "limited self-determination" that applied to all member states of the "socialist commonwealth." Thus, in a major article in *Pravda* (September 26, 1968), entitled "Sovereignty and Internationalist Obligations of

Socialist Countries," the Soviet Communist party ideologist S. Kovalev
stated:

> Just as, in V.I. Lenin's words, someone living in a society cannot be free of that
> society, so a socialist state that is in a system of other states constituting a socialist
> commonwealth cannot be free of the common interests of that commonwealth. The
> sovereignty of individual socialist countries cannot be counterposed to the interests of
> world socialism and the world revolutionary movement. . . .
>
> The weakening of any link in the world socialist system has a direct effect on all the
> socialist countries, which cannot be indifferent to this. Thus, the antisocialist forces
> in Czechoslovakia were in essence using talk about the right to self-determination to
> cover up the demands for so-called neutrality and the C.S.R.'s withdrawal from the
> socialist commonwealth.   But implementation of such "self-determination," *i.e.*,
> Czechoslovakia's separation from the socialist commonwealth, would run counter to
> Czechoslovakia's fundamental interests and would harm the other socialist countries.
> Such "self-determination," as a result of which NATO troops might approach Soviet
> borders and the commonwealth of European socialism would be dismembered, in fact
> infringes on the vital interests of these countries' peoples, and fundamentally
> contradicts the right of these peoples to socialist self-determination.

To dispose of the objections that the application of this new Soviet
doctrine violated the norms of international law, Kovalev argued that
every law, including international law, is subordinate to the laws of
class struggle.   Consequently, national interests of the members of the
socialist commonwealth must be subordinated to the common interest, as
determined by the Soviet Union. Thus he continues,

> However in the Marxist conception the norms of law, including the norms governing
> relations between socialist countries, cannot be interpreted in a narrowly formal way,
> outside the general context of the class struggle in the present-day world. . . . Those
> who speak of the "illegality" of the allied socialist countries' actions in Czechoslovakia
> forget that in a class there is and can be no such thing as a nonclass law. Laws and
> norms or law are subordinated to the laws of the class struggle and the laws of
> socialist development.

Finally, on November 12, 1968, Brezhnev restated these arguments in
what has since become known as the Brezhnev Doctrine:

> The experience and struggle and a realistic appraisal of the situation that has taken
> shape in the world also attest very clearly to the fact that it is vitally necessary that
> the Communists of socialist countries raise high the banner of socialist internationalism
> and constantly strengthen the unity and solidarity of the socialist countries. . . . The
> CPSU has always advocated that each socialist country determine the concrete forms of
> its development along the path of socialism by taking into account the specific nature
> of their national conditions. But it is well known, comrades, that there are common
> natural laws of socialist construction, deviation from which could lead to deviation
> from socialism as such. And when external and internal forces hostile to socialism try

to turn the development of a given socialist country in the direction of restoration of the capitalist system, when a threat arises to the cause of socialism in that country—a threat to the security of the socialist commonwealth as a whole—this is no longer merely a problem for that country's people, but a common problem, the concern of all socialist countries.

The promulgation of the Brezhnev Doctrine marked a return to the concept of "proletarian internationalism" as it was understood by Stalin. It also once again transformed the idea of "different roads to socialism," which had become the euphemism for national self-determination within the communist universe, into an anachronism. "Proletarian internationalism" was defined by CPSU ideologist Sovetov in November 1968 as "solidarity with the Soviet state and support of it in the international arena."

Socialists United

The Soviet move into Czechoslovakia rang bells of alarm in the communist countries that were outside or on the fringe of the Soviet embrace, such as Romania, Yugoslavia, China, and Albania. Brezhnev's discarding of the "different roads to socialism" theory posed a direct security challenge to them. On the day of the invasion, August 21, Nicolai Ceausescu addressed a rally in front of the Romanian Communist Party headquarters, declaring:

The penetration of the troops of the five socialist countries into Czechoslovakia is a great mistake and a grave danger to peace in Europe, to the fate of socialism in the world. It is inconceivable in the world today, when the people are rising to the struggle for defending their national independence, for equality of rights, that a socialist state should transgress the liberty and independence of another state. There is no justification whatsoever and no reason can be accepted for admitting for even a single moment the idea of military intervention in the affairs of a fraternal socialist state.

One of the more troubling aspects of the Soviet move was the setting up of a rival puppet regime and then legitimating intervention as a response to a call for assistance from that same puppet regime. Presumably, the Kremlin could now feel free to repeat this ploy in any "socialist" country, and indeed, particularly in a state ruled by a communist maverick like Ceausescu. The Romanian president took a strong stand on this issue the very next day in an address to an extraordinary session of the Romanian parliament:

The troops of the five socialist countries entered Czechoslovakia without having been called by the elected, constitutional, legal bodies of the country, under the pretext of an appeal made by a certain group. However, in the whole international life, it is unanimously known and accepted that relations between parties and states are established exclusively between the legal leaderships of the same and not between groups or persons who do not represent anybody. To admit the abandoning of the principles, the introduction of the practice to invoke for one or another action the requests of isolated groups, means to open the road to arbitrariness, to help towards intervention in the affairs of other parties or states, including the military occupation of some countries.

On August 22, the government of the Socialist Federal Republic of Yugoslavia (SFRY) issued a formal statement that largely reiterated the Romanian position:

The armed intervention of the above-mentioned group of countries, which was carried out without the invitation and against the will of the government and other constitutional organs of the Socialist Republic of Czechoslovakia, represents the most brutal trampling down of the sovereignty and territorial integrity of an independent country, as well as a plain negation of the generally accepted principles of International Law and of the United Nations Charter.

The Government of the SFRY feels that no state, or group of states has the right to decide on the fate of another country or on its internal development, or to undertake measures which are in contradiction to the publicly expressed will of the people and constitutional organs of that country.

Moreover, on March 12, 1969, President Tito issued an unambiguous rejection of the Brezhnev Doctrine and its limitation on the integral sovereignty of members of the socialist community of states:

In some East European socialist countries the unacceptable doctrine of a "collective," "integrated," and of an essentially limited sovereignty, is appearing. In the name of a supposedly higher level of relationships between socialist countries, this doctrine negates the sovereignty of these states and tries to legalize the right of one or more countries according to their own judgment, and if necessary by military intervention to force their will upon other socialist countries. Naturally, we reject decisively such a concept as contrary to the basic rights of all nations to independence and contrary to the principles of international law.

The Central Committee of the Albanian Communist Party issued a statement on August 22, declaring that

the Warsaw Treaty has ceased to be a pact protecting the socialist countries which are signatories to it. . . . From a peace treaty, the Warsaw Treaty has been turned into a treaty of war for enslavement. From a treaty of defense against imperialist aggression, it has been turned into an aggressive treaty against the socialist countries themselves.

On March 17, 1969, the *People's Daily* of Beijing noted that

"limited sovereignty" in essence means that Soviet revisionism can encroach upon the sovereignty of other countries and interfere in their domestic affairs at will, and even send its troops into the territory of these countries to suppress the people there, while the people invaded have no right to resist aggression and safeguard their own sovereignty and independence. This is an out-and-out fascist "theory."

Lin Biao of the People's Republic of China pointed out unequivocally the implications of the Brezhnev Doctrine, implications that are even more pertinent today. On April 1, 1969, in his report to the Ninth Congress of the Chinese Communist Party, he stated:

In order to justify its aggression and plunder, the Soviet revisionist renegade clique trumpets the so-called theory of "limited sovereignty," the theory of "international dictatorship," and the theory of "socialist community." What does all this stuff mean? It means that your sovereignty is "limited," while his is unlimited. You won't obey him? He will exercise "international dictatorship" over you—dictatorship over the people of other countries, in order to form the "socialist community" ruled by the new tsars, that is, colonies of social-imperialism.

The Brezhnev Doctrine was indeed an attempt at providing a legitimating rationale for Soviet imperialism. What was uncertain at the time of its promulgation was whether it extended beyond Eastern Europe and the Warsaw Pact signatories. It would take another decade to get the answer to this question.

WESTERN RESPONSE

In the United States and other industrial democracies, the implications of the Brezhnev Doctrine were soon submerged in the new spirit of détente that emerged in the early 1970s. In December 1975, at a meeting in London of U.S. ambassadors in Europe, Helmut Sonnenfeldt, counselor to the State Department, made a number of remarks to the assembly that outlined U.S. national security policy with regard to the Soviet Union in a period of détente. In the course of his defense of the détente policy, according to the official State Department summary, he made the following statement on Eastern Europe that subsequently became known as the "Sonnenfeldt Corollary to the Brezhnev Doctrine":

With regard to Eastern Europe, it must be in our long-term interest to influence events in this area—because of the present unnatural relationship with the Soviet Union—so that they will not sooner or later explode, causing World War III. This inorganic, unnatural relationship is a far greater danger to world peace than the conflict between East and West. . . .

So it must be our policy to strive for an evolution that makes the relationship between Eastern Europeans and the Soviet Union an organic one. Any excess of zeal on our part is bound to produce results that could reverse the desired process for a period of time, even though the process would remain inevitable within the next 100 years. But of course, for us that is too long a time to wait.

So our policy must be a policy of responding to the clearly visible aspirations in Eastern Europe for a more autonomous existence within the context of a strong Soviet geopolitical influence. This has worked in Poland. The Poles have been able to overcome their romantic political inclinations which led to their disasters in the past. They have been skillful in developing a policy that is satisfying their needs for a national identity without arousing Soviet reactions. It is a long process.

A similar process is now going on in Hungary. János Kádár's performance has been remarkable in finding ways which are acceptable to the Soviet Union, which develop Hungarian roots and the natural aspirations of the people. He has conducted a number of experiments in the social and economic areas. To a large degree he has been able to do this because the Soviets have four divisions in Hungary and therefore have not been overly concerned. He has skillfully used their presence as a security blanket for the Soviets, in a way that has been advantageous to the development of his own country.

This remarkable statement, which truly reflects the requirements of a lopsided policy of détente, implied U.S. acceptance of the Brezhnev Doctrine and Soviet imperialism. Poland and Hungary were presented as models of how East European states may achieve "a more autonomous existence within the context of a strong Soviet geopolitical influence" without reference to such matters as sovereignty, independence, or self-determination.

It is not at all surprising that with the official complacency with regard to Soviet domination of Eastern Europe, as reflected by the Sonnenfeldt Doctrine, the Kremlin might consider that it would be equally acceptable if the Soviet empire went through some further expansion, a development that was not long in coming. What is surprising is that so little attention was being paid to what the Soviets were doing and saying that contradicted détente.

BOLD SOVIET MOVES

In May 1974, Soviet Defense Minister Marshal Andrei Grechko sent an unmistakable signal of Soviet intentions with regard to the possible range of application of the Brezhnev Doctrine. He stated:

In the present stage, the historic function of the Soviet armed forces is not restricted merely to their function of defending our Motherland and the other Socialist countries. In its foreign policy activity, the Soviet state actively and purposefully opposes the export of counter-revolution and the policy of oppression, supports the national liberation struggle, and resolutely resists imperialist aggression in whatever distant region of our planet it may appear.

Afghanistan

Complacency with regard to the Brezhnev Doctrine began to fade with the April 1978 coup that brought a Marxist government to power in Afghanistan. In December of that year, the USSR and Afghanistan entered into a Treaty of Friendship, Good Neighborliness, and Cooperation. As the insurgency against the Marxist government developed, Soviet involvement in the country to bolster the regime mounted, culminating in the invasion of Afghanistan in December 1979. Shocked by this first use of the Soviet army outside of Europe since World War II, the apologists and the ingenuous were quick to provide a restrictive rationale for this blatant application of the Brezhnev Doctrine in Asia. Afghanistan is, after all, contiguous with the Soviet Union's southern border. Consequently, it was argued, there was no basis for assuming that the Soviets would contemplate seriously the extension of the scope of the Brezhnev Doctrine to noncontiguous regions such as Central America, Africa, or Southeast Asia.

The naïveté of this formulation was demonstrated on January 18, 1980. On that date, a new and updated version of the Brezhnev Doctrine appeared in the Moscow weekly *Novoye Vremya*, which stated in part:

> The question arises: What is the international solidarity of revolutionaries? Does it consist only of moral and diplomatic support and verbal wishes for success, or does it also consist, under justified, extraordinary conditions, in rendering material aid, including military aid, all the more so when it is a case of blatant, massive outside intervention?

> The history of the revolutionary movement confirms the moral and political rightness of this form of aid and support. This was the case, for instance, in Spain in the '30s, and in China in the '20s and '30s. Now that the system of socialist states exists, to deny the right to such aid would simply be strange.

Consistent with the logic of this pronouncement, any country in any part of the globe that proclaimed communist goals would not only be eligible for Soviet military assistance but also might find itself subject to intervention to protect its earlier revolutionary gains, as had occurred only three weeks earlier in Afghanistan.

Cuba

Approximately one year later, the Brezhnev Doctrine was unquestionably extended beyond territories contiguous to the USSR, beginning with Cuba. Since Cuba has no formal military pact with the Soviet Union,

Fidel Castro exhibited some uneasiness regarding possible actions against him by the United States in consequence of the administration's charges regarding Cuba's involvement in El Salvador. Speaking to the Soviet Communist Party Congress on February 25, 1981, Castro declared:

> Ninety miles from our fatherland are those who proclaim the need to destroy us. We are openly threatened with military blockade, and even more drastic measures are studied with the aim of obliterating the example of socialist Cuba from Latin America and of punishing the Cuban people for their friendship with the USSR and the socialist community.

Although Castro's obvious plea for Soviet reassurance was downplayed publicly, Brezhnev's response came, almost as an aside, during a speech in Prague on April 7. He declared that

> the glorious Republic of Cuba, an inseparable part of the community of socialist states, is fulfilling the tasks of its development under difficult external conditions. The Soviet Union firmly and invariably supports and will continue to support the fraternal Cuban people.

The explicit identification of Cuba as "an inseparable part of the community of socialist states" clearly makes it subject to application of the Brezhnev Doctrine. This includes a commitment to use Soviet military power in Cuba, even in the absence of a formal military pact.

On November 6, Soviet defense minister Dimitri Ustinov warned the United States to take account of the consequences of any punitive actions against Cuba. This implicit threat was carried even further on November 17 by the following statement in *Izvestia*:

> The organizers of the anti-Cuban provocations should be clearly aware of the dangerous consequences of their actions. Cuba is a member of the socialist community . . . in the difficult conditions of confrontation with imperialism, their true friends and likeminded people are by their side.

In October 1983, an article entitled "Important Milestone in the History of Soviet-Vietnam Relations" appeared in Moscow's *Kommunist* in anticipation of the fifth anniversary of the signing of the USSR-Vietnam Treaty of Friendship and Cooperation on November 3, 1978. The article noted in part that the treaty was based "on the inviolable principles of Marxism-Leninism" and "proletarian internationalism," and stated that the treaty

> effectively serves the peaceful constructive toil of our peoples, and the protection of their revolutionary gains from any outside encroachments. All forces of imperialism and reaction must take its influence into consideration, whether they wish it or not.

Thus, one may reasonably conclude that the Brezhnev Doctrine now applies to Vietnam as well.

Given that the Brezhnev Doctrine has now ostensibly been made applicable in the Western Hemisphere, is it safe to assume that only Cuba comes under its sway? It is well worth noting that on December 7, 1981, the Soviet ambassador to Nicaragua stated, "In case the American government should decide to attack Nicaragua, the USSR, which has supported Nicaragua, is going to support it in its struggle for peace, security, defense, and for its reconstruction." While his statement is sufficiently ambiguous to allow a variety of interpretations, it does contain the hint of the Soviets' readiness to bring the Marxist regime of Nicaragua under the umbrella of the Brezhnev Doctrine at some point in the not too distant future, perhaps once the present crisis is resolved. In the final analysis, the extension and application of the Brezhnev Doctrine in Latin America may be delimited only by Soviet and Cuban capability to act militarily.

Similarly, the prospect increases that, given the military wherewithal and an accurate assessment of Western weakness, the USSR will feel a greater willingness to initiate and then intervene in coups d'état, revolutions, ongoing rebellions, and local wars. By recognizing one group as legitimate and providing it with credibility via a sudden injection of Soviet forces, the USSR would be able to unilaterally expand its domain while simultaneously inflicting a body blow on Western interests and American prestige. No doubt, this kind of imperialism will be carried out by surprise, presented as a *fait accompli*, cloaked by dissimulation, aided by endorsements from grateful Soviet clients, and justified in the name of "legitimate Soviet security concerns."

In essence, one can expect that the Soviet Union is now prepared to apply the Brezhnev Doctrine wherever it can. In such instances, the USSR certainly will mount an aggressive campaign of justification, backed by the threat of further military aggression yet camouflaged by pledges of peaceful intent and denials of further ambitions. In the Soviet strategy, the net effect will be to make the next round of expansion even easier and even more justifiable.

CHAPTER 4

Soviet Strategizing

The Free World and the Soviet imperium are locked in continuing protracted conflict. This is not of the Free World's choice; none of its members seeks conflict or conquest. But neither is there any evidence that the Free World's response up to now has in any way deflected the Soviets from their determination to keep on waging their multipronged war against it. Having discussed in chapter two the cultural and political characteristics that distinguish the Soviet threat, let us consider aspects of Soviet strategy and Soviet strategizing.

The Soviets' ultimate objective is global hegemony. The sheer scope of Soviet ambitions sometimes makes it difficult for us to fathom the true dimensions of the Soviet threat. In fact, the Soviet Union's own definition of its identity makes anything less than global hegemony a logical contradiction.

The Soviet Union defines its enemies on the basis of so-called class distinctions. It has established itself as the avant-garde of history's drive for class struggle, culminating in a proletarian revolution and assertion by the proletariat, through the CPSU, of the dictatorship of the proletariat. As a totalitarian Russian oligarchy, imbued with the belief that it possesses the mandate of heaven (or history) to exercise global leadership and thus global proprietorship, the USSR is organically incapable over the long term of sharing either political or ideological power. The Soviet Union, deferring to its own military limitations or tactical needs, does assume less than total domination as a matter of course. But this in no way means that Soviet objectives are any less encompassing or that they would be moderated if the Soviet leadership did not feel restraint was a practical necessity.

One can see evidence of this in the way the USSR operates military bases abroad. In every instance where the USSR has been able to gain

31

base rights, it has sought total control of the military bases, even to the point of extra-territoriality. In Somalia and Egypt, this reach elicited an unwelcome reaction by the still-independent local governments: the USSR was forced out of bases at Berbera and Alexandria. Yet in Iraq, South Yemen, Cuba, Vietnam, and Grenada, the USSR continued the pattern of seeking total control. A similar approach was observed on a political basis in Afghanistan. The coup that brought the KGB puppet Babrak Karmal to power in 1979 was organized by the Soviet Union when it felt that the previous Afghan communist leader Hafizullah Amin was insufficiently responsive.

The Soviets operate as close to this fashion as possible in the Warsaw Pact, in part because the Soviets distrust their own allies. The larger message of the USSR's suppression within the Eastern bloc—in East Germany in 1953, Hungary in 1956, Czechoslovakia in 1968, and Poland in 1980—has been that wherever the USSR can exercise hegemony it will do so, and it will back up its position by unlimited violence if necessary.

The Soviet timetable is flexible and open-ended. Soviet leaders never have made a secret of their global strategic objective or of their tactical flexibility. Even before the 1917 Bolshevik Revolution and later, from Lenin to Mikhail Gorbachev, by word and by deed they have made their strategic design brutally apparent while facilitating its progress wherever opportunities arose and with whatever tactics proved most effective and, if possible, most deceptive.

SIZING UP OPPONENTS

The Soviet global strategy involves many players and proceeds by many vehicles: only rarely with the direct use of Soviet force, more often with the use of force by surrogates (complemented by Soviet and surrogate "advisers to indigenous power wielders"), most often and increasingly by threat and intimidation. The Soviet arsenal also includes a wide range of weapons of unconventional or low-intensity warfare—political, psychological, economic, and diplomatic. It extends to state-sponsored terrorism and to traffic in drugs and arms. The crisis now confronting the Free World has largely been brought about by a massive twenty-year Soviet buildup in every sphere of conflict, including space. Yet undergirding the entire Soviet strategic design is Soviet military power, both conventional and nuclear, growing ruthlessly in its various configurations from rough parity with the Free World to clear superiority to outright monopoly.

The Soviet Union counts as part of its strategy the continuing absence among the targets of its imperialism any collective understanding or acknowledgment that they are under general attack. The Soviet Union confronts the Free World with a single, conscious global strategic design, yet it utilizes and promotes division within the Free World so that the scope of that design does not become an element in the Free World's response. This means, in turn, that each firefight, each threat and instance of intimidation, each Soviet political offensive, each new wave of state-sponsored international terrorism, each disinformation campaign and propaganda ploy is seen as an isolated phenomenon. The Free World's response to these tactics has been sporadic and disjointed, and this is precisely the reaction the Soviets have tried to elicit. Their realistic understanding has been that Soviet aggression would certainly elicit some defensive response, so minimizing this response and its duration then should be part of the Soviet design.

DISPARATE APPROACHES TO CONFLICT

The United States and the Soviet Union are not only divided by fundamentally different approaches to the nature of governance and individual rights, they also are divided strategically by differing concepts of time, engagement, levels of conflicts, and strategic and tactical achievement. Therefore, the Soviets think in terms of processes, and they view American failures in terms of the weak American strategic processes thus illuminated. Given this, the Soviet Union is apt to challenge the United States in a number of areas with similar tactics until it becomes clear that the United States has changed its strategic processes and not just its local theater tactics.

This reality operates on several levels. The Soviet Union pursues various aspects of its strategy in several ways and at numerous times in order to reveal or test different systemic weaknesses of the United States. Heretofore, this aspect of Soviet imperialism has hardly been addressed. It is now clear that any act of Soviet adventurism is performed in two theaters: first, the local arena where the politics of the matter are played out; and second, the intellectual theater, where America's handling of the local or regional problem is analyzed for insights about how effectively or ineffectively the United States performs. Thus, even a local failure for the Soviet Union may reveal weaknesses that can be exploited for future success.

For example, on a propaganda level, the Soviets view arms control negotiations as a way of improving their image and influence in the world. On a true strategic level, they view these negotiations as a way of solidifying their strategic advantages over the West. But the Soviets also perceive arms control negotiations as a device that reveals the way in which certain intelligence and national estimate agencies of the

United States work, as well as how influential they are and with whom. Similarly, Soviet naval expansion in Vietnam, for instance, not only promotes the Soviet position in Southeast Asia, but it also forces the United States to reveal some of its naval strategy and tactics and thus the underlying views and processes of the American military and political leadership. Because of their utility worldwide, these kinds of strategic harvests may be as fruitful for the Soviets in the long run as direct gains in a particular theater.

The United States tends to look at conflicts as if their implications and costs were confined to one region. This is the obverse of the previous point. But an American setback in Lebanon, for instance, can have a measurable, deleterious effect on American policy in far-flung regions. It can encourage the Soviets to employ similar tactics elsewhere on the assumption that the mechanism that brought success in one region may be applicable in others (and may elicit the same initial, ineffective American response). Thus, for the USSR, tactical insights, just like systemic insights, are strategically fungible and transferable. But, as discussed later in this book, the overcompartmentalized American approach to both global strategies and regional tactics prevents us from gleaning as much from our tests and assessments of Soviet behavior.

Not only does the United States think in terms of regions and localized issues, but it views conflicts as staged in an immediate time frame. In contrast, the USSR has a much longer time frame and looks for underlying trends in disparate regions and theaters, seeking to capitalize on them. The United States, on the other hand, tends to view conflicts as geographically and temporally discrete. Similarly, the United States perceives victories as permanent and conflicts as soluble in one fell swoop, whereas the USSR, taking the longer view, is willing to try again and again after complete defeat (as in Egypt) or a major setback (as in Sudan and Somalia).

The Soviet Union increasingly recognizes that it cannot be permanently barred from any region, despite setbacks. This is because the Soviet presence is not contingent upon trade and because the Soviet Union has established itself as a superpower that cannot be threatened past a certain point. In some places today, such as Iran and Lebanon, the United States faces the prospect of being completely barred as a result of unremitting and unchallenged terrorism. Not only does the USSR not face this threat, it has within its power the ability to make this threat to the United States grow via its covert support for international terrorists such as the PLO and Libya's Colonel Quaddafi.

It must be borne in mind (as demonstrated in Iran) that Soviet strategy, while favoring the establishment of communist regimes, is perfectly willing to promote and accept the removal of pro-Western regimes and their replacement by neutral or anti-Western (if not necessarily pro-Soviet) governments. Because the USSR judges the balance of its war against the West on a net asset basis, any diminution of the Western position is welcomed on the assumption that by definition it advances Soviet interests and sets the stage for the further expansion of Soviet hegemony.

The Soviets recognize that the key concern should not be the numbers of the strategic nuclear equation but rather the political effect and implications that a *general* position of inferiority has upon the United States. The Soviet Union makes this assessment on the basis of the overall strategic and conventional equation, judging in both major and minor arenas whether the United States can be threatened or intimidated and whether the USSR feels freer to move more aggressively and with greater confidence in the face of seemingly greater risks. Willing to probe almost anywhere opportunity arises, whether there is a prospect of a major payoff or not, the Soviet Union operates under the following assumptions:

1) America's confidence to act worldwide can be undermined by local preoccupations;
2) America's general responsiveness can be slowed if the United States is progressively encumbered with ever greater numbers of political arenas in which it must show leadership and for which it must assume responsibility; and
3) strains applied in any arena, even a minor one, may reveal systemic American shortcomings that may have a deleterious effect on American interests in other, more critical theaters.

Micronesia—the Pacific archipelago in trusteeship to the United States since World War II—is one target of Soviet strategy in this regard. Recent Soviet moves there have been designed to merely establish a psychological presence, yet one that the United States must take into account. Further, Soviet entry there communicates to Washington the fact that the United States has taken for granted the strategic position it has in the South Pacific; a dot on the map, after all, does not constitute a strategic defense line. So here, the most effective Soviet strategy has not been so much a planned initiative with long-term goals but rather a reactive counterstrategy designed to unsettle the United States and force a reallocation (and concomitant thinning) of America's assets. Here, then, we see how Soviet strategy may be aimed at nothing more (or less) than the straining of American strategic resources and thus the acceleration of its defeat.

DIVERSIONARY TACTICS

The Soviets also try to force the United States to make tactics into strategies. Arms control is a textbook example of this. Arms control has become a diversion, something to take the place of an overall strategy and to serve as a substitute for a foreign policy. More properly seen as one diplomatic instrument among many, arms control as a strategy is handicapped by the fact that it tends to focus attention onto esoterica and away from regional conflicts and broad geopolitical trends and realities. It enables the Soviets to divert American attention away from larger, continuing problems, while the Soviets play the chimera of strategic arms stability in such a way that it activates America's fascination with solutionism.

When arms control diplomacy produces something tangible, the United States takes from the success, such as it is, a false sense of confidence and accomplishment. When the treaties, which are the fruits of such "successes," are implemented or when the achievement of agreement on a treaty seems near, arms control diplomacy has the effect of slowing or even paralyzing the American response to Soviet aggression. The 1973 Soviet connivance with the Arabs and the Soviet airlift resupply during the Yom Kippur War are classic illustrations of this.

Even on a geopolitical scale, arms control diplomacy acts as a diversion and an intimidator. With the emphasis on strategic weapons, the primacy attached to controlling their growth facilitates acceptance of two Soviet arguments: any regional conflict would lead to a strategic (and inevitably nuclear) conflict; and arms control must conform to Soviet definitions in order to be considered "fair." This has the effect of disarming the United States psychologically as well as politically. It also intimidates the Free World in the conventional and regional sphere, while simultaneously allowing the Soviet Union to move with greater certitude and with a carefully honed nuclear-use strategy to promote its aggressive objectives.

For instance, by its statements and actions, the Soviet Union communicates the message that the United States cannot touch Cuba, Libya, or Ethiopia, or we might infringe upon Soviet interests or engage with Soviet troops, inevitably escalating the conflict to the full-scale nuclear stage. In reality, this threat is almost entirely false.

Conversely, the Soviets perceive almost no threat that any of their adventures may escalate into a nuclear confrontation with the United States. They enter their adventures and pursue their plans with a sense that their risks and exposure will be limited, freeing them to take greater chances. They understand that if vital interests of the West are threatened, the United States and its allies will respond by trying to defuse the situation on the theater/regional/local level. Furthermore, the Soviets have determined that even while challenging the USSR in that theater the United States and its allies will not hold the Soviet Union responsible for any imbroglio to the point where the Soviet Union itself becomes directly threatened. The USSR understands that, on the contrary, the West will be at pains to convince the Soviet Union that its concerns are wholly local. Thus, the USSR intimidates the Free World into accepting limitations upon the Western scope of action while it remains free of constraints on its own scope of action.

The Soviets understand that intimidation by Moscow at the strategic level creates more freedom to maneuver at the conventional level. Believing the United States will not or cannot respond, the Soviets then use their conventional weapons to advance their geopolitical-cum-strategic position. Conversely, effective response by the United States on the local level restrains the USSR, to some extent, on both the local and strategic levels. There is much less separation here than conventional wisdom would acknowledge, just as the Soviets see much less separation between strategic and theater conflicts, perceiving differences to exist functionally rather than as a matter of locale and scale.

The Soviet Union shows a tactical flexibility that the United States, despite (or because of) its different intellectual culture, seems incapable of employing. Depending on the mood of the time, the Soviet Union uses political tools, ideological appeals, or economic blandishments to promote its fortunes. It readily exploits the institutional weaknesses of the West, including the propensity of capitalist enterprises to sell to communist states whatever they need and of analysts to see periodic Soviet moves toward pragmatism as evidence of some genuine moderation on a Western model or evidence of a school of moderation fighting for existence against an extremist element within the Soviet leadership.

Soviet strategists reflexively work at the weaknesses and ambiguities of Western public opinion, while protecting areas of Soviet weakness with equal reflexiveness. Throughout, the USSR dissimulates about its actions, motives, and the nature of objective reality. Thus, the USSR will denigrate the effectiveness of economic sanctions, while working feverishly to circumvent those it most fears: the limitation of inflows of capital and technology. Moreover, the Soviets will focus upon Western misdeeds or frequently invent them via disinformation in order to divert attention in Third World nations from the larger aspects of the East-West conflict or local manifestations of Soviet aggression.

Ultimately, the alternating current of Soviet aggressiveness and accommodation has a specifically *strategic* purpose: to cause ideological and intellectual discord within the West, such that no definition of the Soviet threat can be agreed upon and that no long-term counterstrategy can be devised and implemented. The net effect of all this is complex. It enables the Soviets to exacerbate the basic level of local conflict. By virtue of their massive nuclear arsenal and their willingness to support with weapons and diplomatic aid any Marxist party in any local conflict, the general level of international tension is raised while simultaneously creating myriad opportunities for Soviet expansion. This is a remarkably abnormal state of affairs, one that we have come to accept uncritically, yet one that should be challenged intellectually and by a revaluation of strategy.

CHAPTER 5

The Search for
Escalation Dominance

The most important aspect of the Soviet approach to strategy is the pursuit of escalation dominance. The term has a number of interrelated meanings. At its essence, escalation dominance should be defined as the *perceived* physical and psychological ability and willingness on the part of the Soviets to counter any Western initiative or counterstrategy and, in so doing, to raise the perceived cost to the United States and its allies for continuing to challenge the Soviet Union.

The Soviet Union's desire for escalation dominance is crucial, for it illuminates fundamental Soviet and Russian motivations. Moreover, the fact that the Soviet leadership is genuinely intent upon achieving escalation dominance reveals that the goal of the grand strategy of the Soviet Union is indeed world domination. If escalation dominance were not regarded by the Soviet leadership as a realistic possibility, then the West could discount suggestions that the Soviet Union's aggressive goals are ultimately unlimited. But if the West determines that the Soviet leadership is conducting its affairs in such a manner as to constantly increase the perception that the USSR possesses escalation dominance, then the grand strategy of the USSR must be regarded as being every bit as menacing as its most committed opponents have claimed.

Aside from the consideration of grand strategy, there are other motivations behind the Soviet Union's pursuit of escalation dominance. The first motivation is one that the Soviet government shares with history's other great aggressors: Escalation dominance allows a nation to minimize the political, financial, diplomatic, and military outlays it must make for its political acquisitions. The Soviets are not the Assyrians or the Mongols; that is, they do not relish bloodshed and the clash of arms for their own sake. The Soviets wish to acquire what they can as inexpensively as they can. In this regard, they wish to

39

possess escalation dominance in the same manner as any bully and to be able to assert their primacy and gain the associated benefits merely by the use of threats.

The second motivation is a matter of compensation. As Soviets and as Russians, the leaders of the USSR are afflicted with feelings of inferiority toward the West. This operates on both a technical and social level; it has been an element of Russian consciousness for centuries. At the same time, Russian nationalism posits the innate, spiritual superiority of the Russian state; divine sanction for its actions; and the dangerous, polluting qualities of its adversaries. In this context, the wielding of escalation dominance allows the USSR to achieve the respect due it while demonstrating its long-denied natural superiority over its adversaries.

Allied with this is a third factor of the Russians' desire to inspire fear. Authoritarianism has been the natural *modus operandi* of Russian rulers for centuries. Emphasizing the desirability of order, the Russian approach to power stresses the utility of force. In this context, the threat of escalation dominance minimizes the possibility that Soviet power will be challenged and thus assures that the legitimacy of the *nomenklatura*'s right to rule will either be accepted or deferred to indefinitely.

INTERPRETING ESCALATION DOMINANCE

Escalation dominance is a multifaceted reality. Western policymakers must be conscious of these various aspects, precisely because they are certain to encounter them in their real world dealings with the USSR.

An Image-Maker

First of all, escalation dominance is a matter of psychology. If the USSR communicates that it possesses escalation dominance, then it broadcasts a whole series of messages about the ideological nature of its ruling group. The possession of escalation dominance says that this group of leaders is a truly Leninist group, intent upon the continuation of class warfare on behalf of the international proletariat against the class enemy. It also says that the Soviet leadership is committed to the ultimate triumph of class warfare, as defined by Marx and Lenin.

It thus becomes apparent that demonstrations of escalation dominance play not only to an international audience but to a domestic one as well. On the international stage, even a regional demonstration of escalation dominance gives credibility to Soviet *tactics* by showing that, if challenged, gambits will be backed up; to Soviet *strategy* by emphasizing that the USSR pursues its long-term objectives undaunted by counter-moves and setbacks; and to Soviet *grand strategy* by establishing the "unshakable" (to use a favored Soviet adjective) commitment of the USSR to its essential purpose of class struggle under the revolutionary avant-garde of the CPSU and by proving the inevitability of the communist victory.

On the domestic stage, the same action gives an air of credibility, purposefulness, and seriousness to an entrenched and bureaucratized leadership. In a sense, it rallies the troops (this has resonances in the psyches of both the Soviet and Russian personas). Moreover, demonstrations of Soviet commitment boost the objective credibility of the Soviet government among those it rules. Real victories in the real world are a substantive adjunct to coercive credibility; they enhance the Soviet leadership's basic tool of power, its ability to coerce. In an era when the Soviet leadership is perceived by many both at home and abroad to be struggling for answers, a demonstration of escalation dominance intimidates opponents into silence, builds the confidence of the *nomenklatura*, and gives the Soviet ruling group additional freedom to maneuver, both domestically and in the international sphere.

As a matter of commitment, the possession of escalation dominance speaks volumes about the priorities of the Soviet Union; that it even says these things is deliberate. For instance, the unmitigated buildup of Soviet military power reflects the Soviets' desire to possess traditional escalation dominance on the battlefield. But it also communicates the fact that the USSR is willing to subordinate the consumer desires of its population to its perceived military needs. Like the kamikazes, there is an air of commitment bordering on the seemingly suicidal in all this. Here, too, the image created is deliberate, designed to manipulate both domestic and international psychologies. Soviet and Russian historiography and hagiography play a role here, for the scorched-earth retreats against Napoleon and Hitler and the canonization of horrific sacrifice in both wartime and peace demonstrate (both domestically and internationally) that the Kremlin's willingness to fight to the last nonmember of the *nomenklatura* is not simply a matter of words.

Expansion of Tactics

Second, escalation dominance is a matter of tactics and says something about Soviet capabilities for the will to exercise escalation dominance is meaningless without the tools and techniques to do so. In this context, the sheer size and ubiquity of the Soviet military take on a new meaning: Western policymakers and military analysts frequently have been struck by the seemingly random way in which the USSR has pursued a plethora of military technologies. They have been similarly befuddled by the Soviets' willingness to retain older, less-advanced weapon systems in their arsenal and by their eagerness to establish a military presence wherever possible and at whatever level achievable.

But in the pursuit of escalation dominance, a case can be made for this behavior. The sheer variety of weapons and technologies and the very expanse of the Soviet presence send a message that the USSR has the ability to meet any challenge posed by the West flexibly, to exploit any opportunity that arises quickly, and to do so with the right tools. Moreover, the simple presence of Soviet forces carries with it the now-established threat of further Soviet escalation in the area should the initial Soviet salient be challenged. In an absolute sense, much of this is bluff, of course. But because the West is loathe to challenge aggressive Soviet actions, let alone actions that are merely potentially aggressive, the net result for the USSR is an increase of its ability to threaten and coerce, and thus to create *further* opportunities for the expansion of Soviet interests.

The reach and ambition of the Soviet Union have a multiplier effect on the tactical aspect of escalation dominance. If the Soviets find themselves lacking the tools to respond to the West, they have shown that they are willing to juggle assets to protect a recent gain or cement a new acquisition such as in Africa during the 1970s. Unwilling initially to intervene directly in Angola and Ethiopia, the Soviet Union deployed thousands of Cuban troops and weaponry from both Cuba and the Warsaw Pact in order to reinforce pro-Soviet governments. This is one of the economies afforded any empire, but the Soviet Union differs from empires of the past in its ideological willingness to raise the ante in protecting its interests and in possessing the physical means to deploy rapidly the troops and equipment necessary to accomplish its aims.

The Soviet Union's support for international terrorism and its use of unconventional and illegal forms of warfare add to its pursuit of tactical escalation dominance. The USSR's involvement with international terrorists gives it a fineness of opportunity (via single, politically disruptive acts committed by a handful of operatives) at a low political and financial cost. None of these characteristics can be matched by the cruder, traditional tools of political instrumentality, such as the Soviet army. As demonstrated in Turkey via its Bulgarian surrogate, the USSR—at a minuscule cost to itself and with complete deniability—is willing to feed civil terrorism to the point where a Western nation is destabilized and where only the most ambitious measures by the United States in concert with a competent allied government can restore order.

Similarly, support for international terrorism means that the USSR can use the assassination of key individuals to neutralize their political accomplishments and influence. Again, this approach can be utilized by the USSR at low cost and with a high degree of deniability. The assassination attempt on Pope John Paul II fit precisely into this pattern. Moreover, the image of the Soviet Union as a superpower capable of manipulating terrorists provides the USSR with an enormous psychological advantage in dealing with and intimidating its adversaries.

Another example is the Soviet use of "yellow rain" chemical warfare in Afghanistan and through its Vietnamese surrogate in Cambodia. Again, both the actual gain *in situ* and the psychological impact on a worldwide audience may be taken as being of equal importance. The Soviet Union was able to destroy its opponents in the field when other, more conventional, limited tactics were not succeeding. The sheer brutality of the Soviet response demonstrated the depth of its commitment to escalation dominance. The USSR accelerated the spread of famine in Afghanistan to destroy both the *mujaheddin* and its base of support among the Afghan rural populace is another example of escalation dominance deliberately conducted in the most fearsome way possible.

Cold Anticipation

Third, escalation dominance is a matter of expectation. By operating as it has in Afghanistan, Angola, and elsewhere and by demonstrating that it is undeterred by the criticism of the West and (occasionally) the Third World, the USSR has validated the expectation that it will escalate when forced to do so. This expectation operates both within the Soviet ruling group and the world at large. Within the Soviet leadership, the inability or unwillingness of the West and the United Nations to engage in *diplomatic* escalation is evidence that criticism of Soviet action is essentially ephemeral, and the larger designs of Soviet strategy should not be deflected.

Both within the Soviet Union and outside it, the failure of international opinion to change either the brutal quality or ambitions of Soviet behavior reinforces the Brezhnev Doctrine. That is, Western inaction and Soviet success legitimize the once-outrageous claim of the USSR to the right to protect the gains of socialism with whatever means it chooses. And this legitimization takes place within the Kremlin and in the world at large.

The world has come to accept a Soviet Union that poisons, murders, loots, starves, and acts in a genocidal fashion in defense of what it defines as its "legitimate interests." By refusing to be bound by the norms by which most other nations—in particular, those of the democratic West—are judged, by creating its own logic of international behav-

ior, and by validating it through force, the USSR has made the utiliza-
tion of escalation dominance mostly a matter of its own volition and of
its own judgment of what the United States will find unacceptable.

Moreover, the Soviet use of brutality on a mass scale means that
most mid-sized countries never challenge the USSR directly but rely
instead upon the United States to counter Soviet gambits. As with any
single-tactic defense, reliance upon the United States simplifies the
Soviet pattern of attack and creates new strategic and tactical opportunities for further Soviet aggression.

In a similar fashion, the USSR has arrogated to itself the right to
accuse the United States of outrageous crimes, to misrepresent the positions of itself and its adversaries, to engage in disinformation on a mass
scale, and to mislead and misinform in an Orwellian fashion. The unmitigated nature of Soviet information policy also becomes a part of escalation dominance, for having engaged in such shameless frauds as are
well documented, the USSR can back up its moves on the ground with
the implied threat of blackening the reputation, record, and position of
an adversary government in the minds of a gullible local or regional
opinion. Of debatable value taken alone, disinformation acts as a force
multiplier when used in concert with the wide range of Soviet tactical
tools of political warfare. Here, too, Soviet collusion, actively and by
example, in the general devaluing of the world information order has
created something beyond common ground with fellow autocrats. Over
time, it increases the potential effectiveness of the Soviet Union's own
salients against many of the Third World governments that made common
cause with the USSR against "Western domination" of the news media.

Disparaging Targets

Fourth, escalation dominance is a matter of risk assessment, imposed
primarily on the Soviet Union's targets and adversaries. The previous
three factors, taken together, have created a daunting political/psycho-
logical image of the USSR. In considering what otherwise would be
completely justifiable responses, nations must consider Soviet responses.
These responses exist on a sliding scale of probability; each successful
act of Soviet intimidation and each failure of response by a target
nation increases the probability that the USSR will feel free to escalate
the ante with greater speed and force.

In a sense, the pursuit of escalation dominance imposes ever-greater
costs upon those whom the USSR chooses to confront, and the entire
process *feeds on itself*. This last reality is known to the governments
involved and, in turn, it, too, becomes part of the risk assessment
process. The Soviet Union's cultural aggressiveness and brutality, its

ideological carnivorousness, its military resources, and its waxing political confidence all come together in an accelerating spiral of risk-taking and payoffs for the Kremlin. In this context, nations faced with Soviet gambits must consider the likelihood that

- the Soviet Union will outflank any response;
- it will match escalation for escalation;
- Soviet surrogates will be supported longer and with greater assiduity than American surrogates; and
- measured force will elicit (and merit) the riposte of (to use Soviet parlance) a crushing blow.

As part of escalation dominance, the Soviets reflexively talk down or beat down responses to their own salients. The operational effects of this are apparent on several levels. First, it makes an adversary dispirited and, over time, has the effect of dividing the elite of a targeted nation into a squabbling and paralyzed mass. Second, it deters an adversary from committing itself to a response that requires a long-term investment of capital and political credit. Third, denigration of counterresponses adds to the psychological image of the USSR as an unstoppable colossus, with all that confers psychologically on the Russian self-image and on the image of the USSR on the world stage.

Finally, Soviet derogation of countermoves creates an atmosphere in which the Soviets can achieve the fundamental goal of escalation dominance, achieving gains without cost. This is done by creating an atmosphere in which political decisions by the targeted nation come to revolve around how to accommodate and appease Soviet demands. In this context, the process of risk assessment becomes so distorted that the objective becomes avoiding further escalation by the USSR. This, of course, concedes dominance to the Soviets.

The "Bully" Factor

Ultimately, the fifth aspect of the pursuit of escalation dominance—the strategic factor—is designed to change the rules of international affairs. If the USSR can communicate undeniably the reality that to challenge the USSR is to impose ruinous costs upon oneself, without any hope of victory and if the USSR can communicate this in an increasing number of situations, then Soviet world domination will be assured even before—and even without—the marching of Soviet armies. Having demonstrated a willingness to accept ruinous costs and win, the USSR can gradually create an environment in which its expansion appears ineluctable and thus becomes inevitable. Furthermore, in so doing, this policy is validated by its victims as a matter of unavoidable necessity or the lowest price of risk management.

Most troubling in all this is the fact that escalation is finite; that is, it evolves to a zero sum or negative sum outcome. Similarly, the pursuit of escalation dominance is finite: past a certain point, the unchallenged threat and image of an unstoppable Soviet Union must become a reality. Having increased its international expansion to a certain point, the USSR will be in a position to make coercion the everyday rule of international conduct rather than the exception. In this circumstance, the internal Soviet system will truly have become externalized, and the cause of freedom and democracy will be much the poorer for it, if they exist at all.

MECHANISMS

At its heart, escalation dominance is a matter of perception and psychology. To be effective, the possession of escalation dominance must be public. The preparations to achieve escalation dominance are likely to be covert, but the actual acquisition of escalation dominance cannot take place in secret. Strategists contemplating how the Soviet Union is likely to advance its own strategic plans should consider the ways in which escalation dominance may be enunciated. These are the mechanisms of escalation dominance, its strategic facet put into action.

Controlled Demonstration

One way in which the Soviets demonstrate their possession of escalation dominance is through the exploitation of their own imperial assets. This might be called *escalation dominance by controlled demonstration*. In this context, one can better appreciate the utility offered to the Kremlin by its control over Eastern Europe and the authoritarian nature of the internal Soviet system. Within its own borders, or its extended borders in Eastern Europe, the USSR can demonstrate for the benefit of its adversaries what it is willing to do in order to maintain dominance over those who oppose it.

Obviously, the primary motivation of the USSR in crushing Hungary and Czechoslovakia and coopting Poland was the simple maintenance of control (and the concomitant validation of the communist movement's arrogation of the role of vanguard of the workers' revolution). But the Soviets surely were aware that Eastern Europe was also a captive arena before the world audience, a stage on which they could demonstrate the central element of escalation dominance: the will to win and the ability to ignore external criticism and the dissuasion of "incentives."

Moreover, the Soviets appreciate that within the borders they directly control, the USSR can demonstrate its ability to escalate and win by a number of devices such as direct military intervention, duplicity, exploitation of internal divisions, targeting of dissenters, and the reassertion of control under the rubric of internal Communist party reform. The latter is what is being applied by Gorbachev in his current modernization campaign.

Political Action

The Soviets also demonstrate their possession of escalation dominance by *the ambitious scope of political action.* It can be argued with justification that the Soviets are involved in so many areas of the world because they are following a fundamental Marxist-Leninist (and Trotskyite) imperative to foment revolution. This imperative has remained a part of Soviet grand strategy, even though it has often taken a back seat to Stalin's legacy of "Socialism in One Country" and the careful circumspection of the Politburo culture.

But the sheer scope of Soviet activities has a second purpose, one more immediately useful to the Soviet leadership, and has to do with the gradual assertion of Soviet escalation dominance. On the one hand, the enunciation of Soviet interests in far-flung regions translates into a systematic increase in the standing of the USSR as a superpower. Furthermore, it establishes a precedent of interest under which the USSR can inject itself directly or through its surrogates into local and regional affairs. On the other hand, the sheer scope of Soviet activities, carrying with them by definition *the prospect of subversion, revolution, and immunity from external criticism,* imposes upon the United States an ever-greater number of responsibilities.

Ever more encumbered, the United States must inevitably pick and choose among the areas targeted by the USSR, thus creating further opportunities for Soviet aggression in those locales where an American setback or defeat will do systemic damage to Western interests and in those locales neglected by the United States for more pressing needs elsewhere. For the Soviets, committed to the long-term exhaustion of the will and resources of the United States, direct regional gains are but an aspect of a larger strategic goal: the ultimate assertion of escalation dominance over an America no longer capable physically or psychologically of meeting and matching Soviet designs.

Focus on Single Elements

The Soviets often enunciate their possession of escalation dominance by *concentration of effort in a particular sphere.* The textbook example of this is the stockpiling of strategic missiles. For the Soviets, the payoff is the opposite side of the American predicament articulated by the observation, "We build and they build. We stop and they build." In a field such as strategic missiles, the Soviets can achieve escalation dominance merely by recognizing certain institutional realities:

1) A continuing, steady investment in research and new systems, characterized by a relatively small but reliable annual growth rate, will ultimately eclipse an American effort that is tied to the politicized issue of arms control and in which funding (and the commitment to meet the Soviet threat) ebbs and flows.

2) By keeping older missiles in the inventory and assigning them limited but still useful responsibilities—what the Soviets call a superadditive military structure—American capabilities will be stretched thinner, thus exposing certain new areas of vulnerability.

3) The same process of steady buildup, camouflaged by active Soviet arms control diplomacy, will raise the American political investment in arms control, further slowing the American response to the still-increasing Soviet threat.

4) Stretched thin, financially strapped and looking for attractive political answers, the United States can be manipulated into focusing on certain peripheral segments of arms control. America's hope is that an agreement arresting Soviet development of new, first-strike strategic missile systems ultimately may be achieved if smaller steps are taken first. But the Soviets have demonstrated repeatedly that they will not agree to true reductions. The focus on intermediate theater nuclear missiles in Europe has been a typical example of this, and the danger of this negotiating strategy was made clear in 1987 when the operational existence of mobile, railroad-car-launched SS-24 and truck-launched SS-25 intercontinental ballistic missiles (ICBMs) was publicized.

5) At each stage, as measured by *decade-long increments*, the USSR can expect to find itself

   • substantially more powerful on an absolute military basis;
   • increasingly able to control the pace, substance, focus, and definitions of associated diplomacy;
   • possessing an ever-increasing number of strategic, tactical and battlefield options, created by newly revealed vulnerabilities of an increasingly less-capable, financially strapped United States;
   • confronting a United States where the nature and substance of the Soviet threat is both perpetually and periodically the subject of debate and deep, political division; and

- better positioned to reveal by sudden action the changed international balance, characterized by increased Soviet escalation dominance.

Breakout

This last point illuminates a fifth way in which escalation dominance may be enunciated: *by shock or breakout*. Precisely like an earthquake, this is the sudden culmination of facts. It may be years in the making, but a breakout affirms psychologically what is already mostly established substantively: that power has been realigned and that the relative ability to control regional or global events has shifted permanently from one superpower to the other. Breakout—escalation dominance in action—is where the focus of this discussion now turns.

CHAPTER 6

Breakout from the ABM Treaty

The concept of breakout does not exist in a strategic vacuum or in a weapons vacuum. It is tied directly and mortally to geopolitics and regional realities. The United States must focus on how this connection affects and correlates with conventional forces and political events in those regions. While most attention is focused on the classic strategic arena, many of the decisive battles will be fought in local geopolitical spheres and resolved with conventional arms in what are called low-intensity conflicts (though they hardly are for small stakes).

These spheres include such places as Southern Africa, Iran, and Korea, places where if the USSR were to score an unambiguous gain, the global balance of power would be shifted significantly or decisively. (This may be a useful definition for distinguishing regional conflicts that are truly pivotal.) For the United States, the correlation of forces relates to how the Soviet strategic buildup, insufficiently challenged, may fuel Soviet adventurism throughout the world, thus upsetting the geopolitical balance and encouraging further Soviet thrusts on both the grand and local strategic scales.

One must expect breakout to occur wherever the Soviets can pull it off. They will obfuscate the facts and their intentions, as well as use any claim of breakout to indict their accusers as warmongers. The topic of the next chapter, a breakout through Southwest Asia and down to the Indian Ocean, obviously would be a daunting and difficult matter. But if undertaken, as their behavior in the years following the invasion of Afghanistan showed, it would be energetically defended and validated by the Soviets no less than their aggression in Afghanistan.

As noted by Richard Pipes, part of America's problem is an overcompartmentalization of the world and its conflicts. The United States must look at each threat and the appropriate counterstrategy in global terms

51

and on a total-sum basis. We must correlate how local challenges by the Soviet Union can affect the nuclear balance and the overall geopolitical balance. Soviet strategy is global; therefore, we must look at strategy in the whole and, out of all its constituent elements, synthesize the true dimensions of the Soviet threat. We must look at events, trends, and Soviet and Soviet-client activities in each arena and judge how they relate to other Soviet options and opportunities.

The culture of détente and arms control will not deter the Soviets from breakout if they believe an opportunity has arisen. This reality was made clear in the 1970s. Apart from locking the United States into strategic military inferiority via SALT I and SALT II, the *primary* effect of the era of détente registered at the geopolitical level, and the currency of exchange was Soviet violations of America's assumptions. Overreliance upon the "civilizing" nature of détente and arms control negotiations *concedes* escalation dominance. In such a circumstance, the Soviets are certain to raise the level of risk-taking using conventional means and low-intensity warfare to advance in key regions. Their biggest gains were scored in the 1970s despite SALT and détente (*e.g.*, Angola, Mozambique, Ethiopia, Indochina, Nicaragua, and Iran). In 1979, they discarded proxies and invaded Afghanistan in conventional style.

Now the Soviets appear poised to launch a breakout from the 1972 treaty regulating antiballistic missiles (ABMs). The USSR seems ready to erect a nationwide ABM network quickly. As devastating as this might appear, locking the United States into a position of strategic inferiority at the nuclear level, the most damaging effect would be registered at the regional/geopolitical level. This condition of strategic nuclear inferiority would concede strategic escalation dominance. The USSR could assert that it was prepared to match us up the ladder at any level. This, in turn, would raise the level of Soviet risk-taking, in accordance with their perception of a redefined strategic nuclear balance. The more they perceived themselves to be stronger, the higher risks they would be willing to take *in those areas where they perceived a potentially favorable difference in the geopolitical balance*. This would build upon the generally increased level of Soviet confidence that has come as a result of successfully challenging the West in Ethiopia, Angola, Afghanistan, Nicaragua, and so on during the past fifteen years.

Though by conventional definitions an ABM breakout would mainly affect the strategic arena, in a *functional* sense an ABM breakout would be no different from the USSR's involvement in the aforementioned nations of Asia, Africa, or South America. Such a breakout would be an outflanking maneuver, logistically and psychologically, designed to alter permanently the geopolitical balance in favor of the USSR and to diminish concomitantly the power of the United States. It would increase the

Soviet Union's ability to coerce and create new opportunities for further Soviet expansion.   And it would make the next stage of America's defense of the interests of the West more difficult and less likely to succeed, thus setting the stage for further, accelerated expansion of Soviet interests.

ANTIBALLISTIC MISSILES AND THE BREAKOUT THREAT

For two decades the Soviet Union has followed an unswerving commitment to build and improve strategic defenses. The Soviet leadership has spent as much on strategic defenses as on strategic offensive forces, an estimated $90 billion since 1975. The Soviets are conducting an extensive effort to protect their leadership, as well as a major program to develop the technology of high-energy lasers, and they are developing the potential to deploy nationwide defenses against ballistic missiles. Soviet leaders are preparing their military forces for the possibility of actually fighting a nuclear war. Their strategic defenses are designed to protect their leadership and to neutralize the ability of U.S. nuclear forces to prevail in any future conflict. Following are specific indicators of a Soviet breakout.

Development of the Krasnoyarsk Radar

President Reagan has declared the new, large phased-array radar under construction at Krasnoyarsk in central USSR to be a significant violation of the ABM Treaty for both political and military reasons. Politically, it shows that the Soviets are capable of violating arms control commitments even when they know the United States will discover their violation and even as they negotiate toward new agreements. Militarily, the Krasnoyarsk radar goes to the heart of the ABM Treaty. When the treaty was negotiated, large phased-array radars such as that at Krasnoyarsk were recognized as the critical, long-lead-time components of a nationwide defense. For that reason, their orientation and siting were restricted in a way that would prevent their use to establish an ABM defense of the entire national territory.

However, the radar at Krasnoyarsk is located and oriented in violation of the treaty. It is well located for ballistic-missile warning, attack assessment, and ABM target acquisition and tracking, and its location provides excellent impact prediction data for much of the central USSR. When fully operational *before the end of the decade*, the Krasnoyarsk radar will close the final gap in the radar warning-and-tracking network that includes five other large radars and three currently under construction that together form an arc of coverage against ballistic missiles around the territory of the USSR.

According to congressional testimony by a senior official of the Central Intelligence Agency, these six large radars and the three under construction also have the technical capability of performing battle-management functions and would be a key component of a nationwide ballistic-missile defense. The Krasnoyarsk radar would be an integral part of that system.

Whether or not the USSR attempts an ABM breakout, the Krasnoyarsk radar is already an unambiguous expression of the Soviet pursuit of escalation dominance. In a seminal article published in the Summer 1987 issue of *Global Affairs*, Eric H. Thoemmes asserts:

> The Krasnoyarsk radar is situated among three SS-18 and several SS-11 ICBM fields.
> . . . Combined with data obtained from other Pechora-class radars, the Krasnoyarsk
> radar could detect a U.S. counterforce attack on these ICBMs and, with the use of
> triangulation, provide accurate attack assessment. This not only erodes the U.S.
> deterrent posture, it also enhances Soviet counterforce options and provides a more
> enduring protracted war capability.

Dual-use Systems

Under the provisions of the ABM Treaty, the United States and the USSR agreed not to give missile interceptors and radars developed for defense against aircraft the capability of also defending against strategic ballistic missiles or to test them in an ABM mode. But ever since the signing of the ABM Treaty in 1972, there has been evidence of concurrent testing of Soviet air-defense and ABM systems. On a number of occasions, the United States has asked the Soviets to stop such testing. While they stopped briefly on several occasions, they always resumed concurrent testing. The number and frequency of these Soviet violations of the ABM Treaty for more than a decade indicate that Moscow may be preparing to use dual-purpose systems as a major component of an ABM defense of its national territory.

The new, all-altitude surface-to-air missile (SAM), the SA-10, ostensibly an antiaircraft SAM, is considered the main Soviet defense against bombers, cruise missiles, and short- and intermediate-range ballistic missiles, including the Pershing II. The dual-purpose SA-10 may also have some capability against submarine-launched ballistic missiles (SLBMs) and ICBMs. More than sixty sites with more than 2,100 SA-10 interceptor missiles are now operational in the Soviet Union, and work is under way on sites for at least 1,000 more. Over half of the SA-10s are located near Moscow, providing a high-priority terminal defense of the Soviet leadership, command and control, and other key military facilities.

Believed to be even more effective against ballistic missiles is the new Soviet SA-12 dual-capable interceptor missile, which has been tested against tactical ballistic missiles on several occasions and is believed to have considerable capability against ICBMs and SLBMs as well. The SA-12 is effective at altitudes ranging from 300 feet to 100,000 feet, and operation deployments of the SA-12 were begun in 1986. Large numbers of SA-10s and SA-12s could add a significant terminal-defense capability to a nationwide Soviet ABM defense.

The Moscow ABM System

Moscow and the Soviet leadership are protected by the world's only operational ABM system, which the Soviets began expanding and upgrading in 1978. When completed in the near future, the improved Moscow defense will be a two-layer ABM system consisting of long-range improved Galosh interceptors—to destroy strategic missile warheads with nuclear explosions before they enter the atmosphere—and very-high-acceleration Gazelle interceptor missiles to engage within the atmosphere those targets that escape the first layer of defense. This system consists of one-hundred nuclear-armed missiles on reloadable launchers directed by the new, large battle-management radar at Pushkino outside Moscow.

The production lines now producing components for the Moscow ABM defense could be used to prepare for and support the rapid and wide-spread deployment of a nationwide ABM system. The USSR could also commence production under the rubric of "replacements," "upgrades," and "slow reloads" for the Moscow ABM system. This could defuse American objections by forcing U.S. analysts to split hairs over definitions and would provide yet another demonstration of how Soviet actions do not occur in a vacuum but always have an accompanying propaganda shield and public relations cover as part of a larger strategic objective.

Rapid Reload of ABM Launchers

The ABM Treaty limits the number of deployed launchers and prohibits the development of rapid-reload capabilities. Violating that prohibition, the Soviets have tested the Galosh and Gazelle missiles at the Sary Shagan test range, demonstrating a reload-and-refire time of "much less than a day," according to the Arms Control and Disarmament Agency report on Soviet noncompliance dated February 1, 1986. Thoemmes purports that

even excluding the possibility of extra ABM interceptors stored away from their launch sites, the new Moscow system could provide a rapid reload/refire capability far in excess of the one hundred launcher limit of the ABM treaty. In 1983, it was revealed that the Soviet Union was developing and testing a rapid reload system for the SH-08 [Gazelle] hypersonic interceptor.

Aviation Week and Space Technology (August 29, 1983) quoted a U.S. Department of Defense official as saying,

The absence of reload equipment on the surface indicates an underground automatic reload system. This could double or even triple the number of allowed interceptors under the treaty. With the transportable radar [see below], it is enough so that it cannot be reliably retargeted by the U.S.

Thoemmes adds:

Since launchers are not required to be in silos, and an interceptor missile does not require a conventional launcher, clandestine ABM launch sites could easily be established around Moscow or throughout the country, supported by the vast network of presently deployed radars and the rapidly deployable ABM-X-3. . . .

Moreover, according to the CIA, in order to build such a nationwide ABM defense between 1985 and 1990 . . . total defense spending would [have to] increase at about 4 percent per year. This is clearly within Soviet capabilities and a temptingly inexpensive option.

Mobile ABM Systems

The ABM Treaty prohibits the development, testing, or deployment of mobile ABM systems or components, including interceptor missiles, launchers, and radars. Nevertheless, the Soviets have developed and tested ABM components that appear to be mobile, such as the Flat Twin tracking radars for the Moscow ABM system. The nature of these systems means that both they and the facilities where they are produced can be easily camouflaged. By using mobile interceptor missiles and radars, the Soviets could suddenly deploy a large number of ABM components from a Moscow base throughout the country, *assembling* a nationwide ballistic-missile defense system in the time required to finish a single site. The *Wall Street Journal* asserted on February 25, 1988, that

. . . the Soviets are "internetting" their early warning radars with interceptor-guidance radars. They have conducted "hand-off" exercises in which the large phased-array radars like the controversial one at Krasnoyarsk pick up targets and alert the Flat Twin and Pawn Shop mobile radars that guide their SH-04 and SH-08 anti-missile interceptors. This is the key "battle management" function of an anti-missile system.

Second, the Soviets are mass producing the Flat Twin and Pawn Shop radars, though

the ABM treaty limits them to two locations. Similarly, they are mass producing the
SH-08, a relatively new supersonic missile that intercepts warheads within the
atmosphere, with 500 such missiles already produced and 3,000 ultimately projected.
The ABM treaty limits each side to only 100 interceptors with both anti-aircraft and
anti-missile capability.

It has been argued that the small size of such radars as the Flat
Twin tracking radar and the Pawn Shop missile guidance radar that
comprise the ABM-X-3 system makes them unsuitable or of limited value
to a nationwide missile-defense system.

But Thoemmes argues that

the contribution of these small radars to a rapidly deployable nationwide ABM system
is readily apparent. Their ability to be quickly dispersed would add critical redundancy
to a future Soviet ABM system. Such redundancy would add immeasurable survivability
to the overall system and reduce dependence on the limited numbers of large lucrative
targets such as the Pushkino and Pechora-class warning, tracking and battle
management radars.

Clearly, enhanced survivability in such a superadditive system would
make the breakout of a Soviet ABM system more persuasive *politically
and psychologically*, conferring upon the USSR a strong measure of escalation dominance.

Again Thoemmes notes:

With an infrastructure of modern phased-array radars in place, the Soviets would be
able to quickly emplace the smaller, rapidly deployable components of a nationwide
ABM system with little difficulty . . . this would be greatly facilitated if the
interceptor missiles and small modular radars were produced and stockpiled in advance.
Since Soviet production lines for these systems are presently fully operational, it
appears that this is exactly what is taking place.

Passive Defense and Leadership Protection

The Soviets have made substantial expenditures on passive defense
and civil defense. Soviet ICBM silos have been hardened in recent years
against nuclear attack, as have launch facilities and command and control centers. As many as 1,500 hardened, alternative command posts and
relocation facilities have been prepared for more than 175,000 members
of the party and government leadership throughout the USSR. Deep,
underground bunkers and blast shelters are designed to enable the top
leadership to survive a nuclear attack and to assure continuity of
command and of party control in a nuclear war.

TERRITORIAL DEFENSE AND BREAKOUT

Thoemmes observes:

The dynamic synergism between the growing Soviet preemptive counterforce capability
and a comprehensive strategic defense network may soon allow Soviet war planners to
count on significantly limiting damage in case of war and on achieving victory at any
level of confrontation.   Such an awesome capability would certainly embolden the
Soviets in a crisis situation and reduce the deterrent value of U.S. strategic forces.
This would particularly be the case if the Soviet Union feels confident that it can
effectively deal with a degraded U.S. retaliatory attack. The desire to achieve such a
capability is the motivating force behind Soviet disregard for the ABM treaty and
American views of stability and deterrence.

Indeed, Thoemmes reasons, in and of itself, "the conclusion that the
Soviet Union is preparing the base for a nationwide ABM system, and
that even by nominally staying within the limits of the ABM treaty it
could deploy an extremely formidable defense, leaves the United States
with a diminished range of options."

President Ronald Reagan has determined that the Soviet Union "may
be preparing an ABM defense of its national territory" in violation of
the basic objective of the ABM Treaty. The accumulation of evidence
leads to the conclusion that the Soviets are preparing to break out of
the treaty (perhaps using U.S. Strategic Defense Initiative [SDI] work as
a rationale) and deploy a nationwide strategic defense. Such a step
would have profound implications for the North Atlantic Treaty Organization's (NATO) security and the East-West strategic balance. This kind
of breakout would neutralize the U.S. deterrent and could lead to increased Soviet adventurism in the Third World, intimidation of U.S.
allies, and pressure on the United States in areas of confrontation. Its
shock value, fundamentally reordering the geopolitical balance in favor
of the Soviet Union, would be enormous, and its long-term effect would
be manifested not only at the strategic level but repeatedly at local and
regional levels. This hostile correlation of forces in disparate arenas
crucial to the interests of the West would be almost impossible to arrest
or reverse. Such a breakout could even lead to war.

CHAPTER 7

Breakout in Southwest Asia

The Eurasian landmass is simultaneously a major Soviet asset *and* a formidable barrier to the unfolding of Soviet global strategy. Geography and topography have conspired to make it very difficult for Moscow to pursue its ambitions in the Asia-Pacific area. Because of the pattern of imperial expansion undertaken by Russian rulers over a period of some four hundred years, the empire reached the Pacific at inhospitable northern latitudes that made effective power projection very difficult. Communications from European Russia to Eastern Siberia relied primarily on a single-track, antiquated rail line that stretched for thousands of miles, with a good part of it along the Chinese border. With its major Asiatic port of Vladivostok closed part of the year because of ice, even sea communications were difficult to maintain on a regular basis.

None of this, however, was seen as a major deterrent to Soviet expansion in the Pacific Basin in the early post-World War II years. During Joseph Stalin's reign, there was good reason to expect that China, in due course, would become a Soviet satellite, providing Moscow with direct access to the entire eastern periphery of Asia. With the consolidation of the People's Republic of China (PRC) in 1949, Soviet power could be projected directly by land into the Far East. However, while Mao Zedong viewed himself as subordinate to Stalin, his relations with Stalin's successors were quite different. Moscow was no longer the center of the communist world, and the rift with Beijing proceeded to deepen and expand.

After the fall of Nikita Khrushchev, it was no longer conceivable that China would again play a subservient role to the USSR. The Beijing-Moscow axis came apart completely in 1966 with the onset of China's Cultural Revolution. With the Sino-Soviet split, the Soviets were again denied easy access to the Far East, except at northern outlets open only part of the year. It is no mere coincidence that 1966 also marks the point when Moscow launched a major drive to develop Eastern Siberia. By then, even the most wishful thinkers in the Kremlin were compelled to recognize that if Soviet power and influence were to be projected into the Pacific Basin—a region of vibrant economic development, vast resources, and political ferment—it would have to be based on indigenous Soviet resources and capabilities and not those of China.

LINKING WEST TO EAST

This decision did not come easily. It had long been a tenet of Soviet development economics that the exploitation of the vast resources of Siberia east of Lake Baikal to meet Soviet domestic needs or the European export market was economically prohibitive. Strategic considerations alone could justify the enormous investments required to develop Eastern Siberia, including what the Soviets called the "Project of the Century," or the construction of a new, modern railroad—the Baikal-Amur Mainline—to parallel the existing Trans-Siberian Railroad, only between one-hundred miles and three-hundred miles north of the Chinese border for much of its length. This monumental project took more than ten years to complete and involved bringing the railroad across five mountain ranges and seventeen rivers, through four tunnels (one of which is more than nine miles long), and over fifty-eight bridges constructed specifically for the Baikal-Amur Mainline.

This railroad project contributed directly to the development of the Soviet military-industrial infrastructure necessary to sustain Moscow's growing military and naval power in the Far East. But it was also recognized that while the railroads across Asiatic Russia would play a major role in the economic development of Eastern Siberia, they were vulnerable to relatively easy interdiction from the south in time of crisis and conflict. Moreover, despite the Herculean nature of the project, the Baikal-Amur railroad added only a bare lifeline—analogous to a single superhighway—wholly inadequate for the integrated development of Soviet Asia into the European heartland. The Amur railway is designed to feed the ports of Vladivostok and others with raw materials, but it is inadequate for regular transport to Europe. (This is comparable to the situation of the United States, where much of its transcontinental commerce is shipped coast to coast through the Panama Canal for similar reasons of economy.) Consequently, it would be necessary for the Soviets to

- build or secure all-weather ports on the Pacific coast;
- develop a maritime capability for major sea-lifts from Soviet Black

       Sea ports to the Far East;
- achieve the ability to secure those sea-lanes; and
- embark upon an economically and politically integrated plan to develop Soviet East Asia.

To meet the first need, essentially a technical one, the Soviets have undertaken the development of a new all-weather port at Vostochny, east of Vladivostok, that is intended to become the largest, deepest, and most mechanized seaport in the Soviet Union by the end of the century. In addition, Moscow has gained access to facilities at Najin and is seeking additional facilities at Wonsan in southern North Korea, and it has established major naval and air bases at Cam Ranh Bay and Da Nang in Vietnam. Dealing with the other three objectives, however, is a much more challenging undertaking.

Traditionally, Russian and Soviet expansion was dependent on internal lines of communication. They expanded in areas where there was no opposition and where they were in control of their lines of communications. Now, the USSR is being transformed into a maritime power, *as much out of economic necessity as out of military considerations*. Ultimately, the USSR cannot sustain its Pacific Fleet and Vladivostok unless they achieve a self-sustaining East Asia.

Moreover, beyond strategic necessity, development of Soviet Asia demands secure southerly routes of passage. This requires an independent base in East Asia. To develop Soviet East Asia, the Soviets apparently want to utilize the inflow of investment money and technology from Japan. (They have also expressed an interest in Filipino labor and already have had contacts with the Filipinos on this score.) The Soviet leadership appreciates that without this assistance, the USSR will not be able to compete in robotics, communications, or biotechnology.

Clearly, the Soviets are going to be on the economic defensive (from the West) twenty years from now, *unless they can intimidate the democracies to subsidize their economic development and acquisition of high technology*. This would create an atmosphere that would minimize the deleterious effects of the USSR's own shortcomings and maximize the Soviet Union's ability to compensate by getting things on the most concessionary (some would say *tributary*) basis. Such a circumstance would flow from enhanced Soviet dominance of the East Asian region.

Thus, the problem of today, in which the Soviet Union maintains its internal political power at the expense of economic efficiency, is to find a solution *that will facilitate the continuation of the status quo without political or economic reforms*. The Soviets are endeavoring, at minimum, to maintain their ability to dominate as a superpower after having failed to become an "intrinsic superpower" economically and socially. Their task is to be able to maintain themselves as an extrinsic superpower, and even grow as such. This, in turn, must encourage further subsidizing from Western Europe and noncommunist East Asia that should create additional opportunities for Soviet adventurism and expansion.

The USSR has invested six times more in Siberia than in any other economic district. Investments have shifted dramatically, yet it is still easier, cheaper, and more cost effective for the USSR to ship goods and raw materials by sea than by rail to and from Siberia. The USSR's own economic development plans and needs for Siberia thus require a greater reliance upon sea communications and other external lines of communications, which, in turn, mandates the continued emergence of the USSR as a sea power and further Soviet expansion through Southwest Asia.

In addition, as with high-technology industrial skills, the USSR lacks the capability to make the transition to utilize high-technology energy sources. Because of this, the USSR has no likely prospect of being relieved of the reliance upon natural gas and oil. This is due less in part to the state of Soviet science and more to Soviet and Russian psychology and their attitudes toward the free flow of information and technical innovation. Thus, the acquisition of Southwest Asia, especially oil-rich Iran, would be a great strategic prize to the Soviets, relieving them of the naval choke points they now confront in assuring economic communication with Soviet East Asia and providing them with an accessible resource base to fuel their internal economic expansion.

Moreover, despite *perestroika*, the USSR is an economic cripple and is becoming increasingly *less* competitive in the international market. Coming from the power structure, Gorbachev understands the true limitations of the Soviet economy. The dilemma facing the Kremlin is that it cannot move into a twenty-first-century economy without running the risk of sacrificing control. Reform could easily boomerang on both Gorbachev and the leadership as a whole, and as a dynamic process, it is wholly out of character for the Soviets as communists and as Russians.

Yet the Soviet leadership appreciates that, while internally the nation is moving toward collapse, externally it possesses an enormous instrument capable—if used boldly—of delivering a major victory in East Asia, Southwest Asia, or Western Europe. Gorbachev realizes that the first-strike capability now enjoyed by the USSR could be transitory, especially if the United States deploys the weapons of the Strategic Defense Initiative. Gorbachev's dilemma is whether to move now, while the USSR possesses a first-strike superiority, knowing that this advantage may be nullified in three years to five years by the deployment of SDI. With all this in mind, the Soviet leadership now confronts what is both a conundrum and an opportunity: Can the USSR successfully use its military to enhance, fundamentally and radically, its entire economic and political position?

THE SEA-LANE IMPERATIVE

From a grand strategic point of view, in order to set the stage for its evolution into an extrinsic, economically integrated superpower, the Soviet Union has had to become a sea and naval power. But the Soviets must face the problem of maintaining secure sea routes from the Black Sea through the Suez Canal to the Indian Ocean on to the South China Sea. Alternatively, the route runs through the Mediterranean, around Africa, and then to the Indian Ocean and the Far East. In an almost perfect accord with this projection of Soviet strategic and economic necessity, its aggressive outreach to South Yemen, the Horn of Africa, southern Africa, the Seychelles, and into Southeast Asia at Cam Ranh Bay delineates a logical and even inevitable course of empire. Beyond any requirements of strategic denial of Free World trade routes, it is a pattern of strategic *necessity* for a burgeoning global superpower.

As previously noted, Soviet strategic planning for Asia has been further complicated by lack of direct access to a warm-water port on the open seas that would ease the problems of operating over extended supply routes to Soviet Pacific ports. While it is possible to maintain sea communications with the Far East from Soviet Black Sea ports, these sea lines of communications must transit a number of choke points at which they can be readily interdicted. Ships leaving the Black Sea would have to first pass through the Bosphorus and the Dardanelles, controlled by Turkey, a member of NATO. Once through, it would then be necessary to transit the Suez Canal, another choke point under foreign control, and then the Bab el Mandeb Strait before reaching the open waters of the Indian Ocean.

Alternatively, the route from Odessa to Vladivostok is approximately 11,000 miles. Should the Red Sea route be foreclosed, it would be necessary to cross the Mediterranean and pass through the Straits of Gibraltar, another major choke point under the control of a NATO power, the United Kingdom. Then ships would have to navigate the long cape route around Africa to the Indian Ocean before completing the voyage of some 17,000 miles.

The remaining maritime options are even more dismal. Ships from Soviet Baltic Sea ports have to transit the NATO gauntlet of the Danish and Norwegian straits before reaching the North Sea and the Atlantic Ocean, while use of the Barents Sea port of Murmansk for the required logistical mission is hardly imaginable. It thus became essential for the Soviets to reduce the vulnerability of the long Black Sea-Indian Ocean route (in the event a Sino-Soviet conflict precluded the use of the trans-Siberian railroads). Accordingly, the Soviets in the late 1970s began to seek control over the key choke points of the Red Sea route.

Moscow now has close ties with South Yemen and Ethiopia, both Marxist states that sit astride the Bab el Mandeb Strait. In Ethiopia's Dahlak Islands, situated in the southern sector of the Red Sea, the Soviets have constructed an airbase that will give them effective control of the entire region. Coupled with other Soviet bases and facilities from Socotra Island in the Gulf of Aden to the former U.S. base in Asmara, Ethiopia, Moscow is well positioned to control the flow of sea traffic through this vital sea-lane. In addition, the Soviets have been ardently seeking a rapprochement with Egypt, no doubt in part because it controls the northern Red Sea choke point at the Suez Canal.

However, considering that the Suez Canal was closed from 1967 to 1975 as a consequence of Egyptian-Israeli hostilities, the possible recurrence of such a conflict at an inopportune time from the Soviet perspective requires Moscow to extend its influence and presence in the African rimlands along the vital though longer cape route from the Atlantic to the Indian Ocean. It will be recalled that during the period when the canal was closed and the state of Sino-Soviet relations precluded transit through China, the Kremlin was forced to use the longer route around Africa to ship supplies to North Vietnam.

THE ATTRACTION OF BREAKOUT

The classic détentist argument is that the Soviets will eventually emulate Hungary; that the Hungarian model, with its liberalization and departure from central control, will have to be chosen because the Soviet model will fail on its own accord. But breakout by military means to Southwest Asia, combined with, possibly even facilitating, the ultimate economic vassalization of the Western democracies, is an alternative strategy for the Soviets, one that is much more appealing to the Soviet ruling group. From an internal perspective, it would enable them to

1) demonstrate in the face of nay-sayers on both sides of the Iron Curtain the validity of the old Leninist doctrine within the classic Marxist-Leninist arena;
2) similarly demonstrate the validity of Stalinist means within the Stalinist arena;
3) maintain their current system without decentralizing power;
4) strengthen the standing and influence internationally of the current Soviet system;
5) increase the prestige of the Soviet leadership at home and further strengthen the *nomenklatura* domestically;
6) increase the prestige of the Russian ruling group in a domestic

situation in which Russians are increasingly an imperial minority presiding over an ever-increasing majority of Asiatic Soviet citizens (in this context, the Asiatics will be both impressed and *intimidated*);

7) provide the Soviets with the means to combat Great Russian nationalism by demonstrating the value of Russian leadership of a mixed imperial enterprise and by turning Russian attention outward to the most recent conquests and away from xenophobia, mysticism, and anticosmopolitan fears of mongrelization; and

8) facilitate the development of Soviet East Asia without the necessity of political liberalization or the loss of centralized party control. Clearly, such a victory would have a profoundly salutary effect internally upon the USSR.

Externally, a military breakout would forge a new correlation of *economic* forces, and this fact makes the possibility of such an endeavor especially appealing to a Marxist-Leninist government. In addition, such an external victory would be a traditional way by which Russian governments validate themselves internally and solidify their control. External aggression thus holds the promise of internal validation, the maintenance of internal control, and the reinvigoration (to some extent, short and intermediate term) of the USSR's internal economic well-being.

More importantly, if the Soviets were to acquire a land and political corridor, oil and gas reserves, and warm-water ports on the Persian Gulf and/or Indian Ocean, they would be relieved of the strategic dilemmas and economic limitations they currently face. With such a breakout, the Soviets would achieve a number of goals:

- unilaterally alter the geostrategic balance;
- assert their domination in the Persian Gulf and Southwest Asia;
- markedly diminish the power-projection capabilities of the United States;
- complicate by a quantum degree America's defense of Western interests;
- accelerate the willingness of the Western industrial democracies to become as a matter of survival economic vassals of the Soviet Union;
- increase the coercion quotient of Soviet activities in regions far removed from Southwest Asia;
- reinvigorate the image and stature of the current Soviet leadership throughout the world; and
- create new opportunities for further Soviet adventurism and expansion.

Thus, to break out of Eurasia east of the Urals would be to acquire a straight path to the Indian Ocean through the Iranian-Afghan-Pakistani corridor of Southwest Asia. It thus should be recognized that the invasion of Afghanistan was but the logical first step of a larger process: the fulfillment of Soviet grand *economic* strategy and grand *political* strategy. Soviet domination of Iran and/or Pakistan (or their dismantling, with parts being coopted/incorporated into the Soviet orbit) —or, more easily achieved, forced accommodation by either or both to guaranteed Soviet access via the land route to the Indian Ocean—clearly must be the ultimate objective.

Accordingly, the area of greatest instability must now be regarded as Southwest Asia. Similarly, on the basis of providing the greatest utility to the USSR then, the area of greatest instability must be judged to be Southwest Asia. It is here, in Soviet Central Asia, that Moscow has assembled its greatest preponderance of military strength. Although the thirty Soviet divisions in this region are dwarfed by both its European and Far Eastern deployments, it is in South Central Asia that Soviet force is overwhelmingly superior to any Free World countervailing capability—on land, the countervailing force is precisely zero—notwithstanding U.S. naval power in the region.

These strategic considerations gave new impetus to the age-old Russian ambition to gain direct access to a warm-water port on the Indian Ocean from Russian Central Asia. It is from this standpoint that Iran looms so large in Soviet aims in Southwest Asia. Access through Iran or even Baluchistan to the Indian Ocean would dramatically reduce the present major logistical problems faced by the Soviets in maintaining their Pacific and Indian Ocean fleets and would greatly enhance the operational significance of the Soviet bases in Vietnam. Their current position in Afghanistan places the Soviets within striking range of accomplishing this important strategic goal. With the planned infrastructural development of Eastern Siberia, the stage would be set for the achievement of the primary Soviet ambition in Asia of unchallenged hegemony.

For the Kremlin, the key consideration is *unimpeded access under Soviet control*. This is tied inextricably to the maintenance of Soviet internal control, Soviet economic development and the projection of Soviet power. For all these reasons, those who cite the Soviet experience in Afghanistan as a reason why the Soviets would not attempt a breakout to the Persian Gulf ought to reconsider. The stakes and promised payoff for the USSR are so great that a carefully defined set of territorial objectives, reinforced by a much larger commitment of forces than the Soviets have been willing to make in Afghanistan, would enable the Soviets to achieve and consolidate their victory.

When considering the Soviet perspective on a Southwest Asia breakout, however, the operant region of analogy should be Eastern Europe, not Afghanistan.   The political payoff alone, measured in terms of dramatically increased Soviet ability to intimidate and extract economic and political tribute, would make such an adventure worth the considerable economic and political investment.

This last point illustrates why this question is of special note to the United States in 1988, for the next president has to be aware of the situation he will encounter.   America is coming to a cusp, which will be shaped in part by what the president does or does not do early in his term.   Just as the Soviets have moved with ever-greater boldness each time the United States has failed to repel their diplomatic and military probes, so the next president must be aware that his first decisions may determine whether the Soviets attempt a breakout in Southwest Asia or postpone it indefinitely (as they did with the preemption against China's nuclear facilities a decade ago).   Early on, the next president must respond boldly, in order to force the Soviets to retreat from their plans, lest they precipitately move past the commitment point.

CHAPTER 8

Balance of Power in East Asia

From the perspective of the global balance of power, the emerging theater of primary contention in Asia is the Pacific Basin, a region that already surpasses Europe in economic significance for the United States. With the rapid rise in geopolitical importance of this vast expanse from the Persian Gulf to the China seas, the challenge for the United States is to devise a strategic framework that assures the continued independence and growth of the nations of Asia and the Pacific Basin. Ultimately, the United States and its Asian allies must keep the region free from the sudden assertion of Soviet hegemony.

REGIONAL MILITARY DEPLOYMENTS

For the past decade, the USSR has been engaged in an unprecedented and unrelenting military buildup in Northeast Asia. This aggressive regional salient responds to *no local threat*, nor does it seek to achieve objectives limited to Northeast Asia. Rather, this buildup is intrinsic to and cannot be understood apart from the Soviet drive for global hegemony. The Soviet threat is seamless, and so must be the target's response.

Additionally, the USSR has deployed east of the Urals 150 SS-20 intermediate-range ballistic missiles with nuclear warheads and twenty-five ballistic-missile submarines in Northeast Asian waters. Just recently, the USSR has placed nuclear-capable systems on one of the islands north of Japan that the Soviet Union has occupied since the end of World War II. In addition, the USSR now maintains in the Eastern Soviet Union fifty-three Red Army divisions, stationed mostly along the Sino-Soviet border. On the Kurile Islands of Etorofu and Kunashiri, still claimed as part of Japan's Northern Territories, the USSR has stationed a motorized infantry division of 13,000 men and forty supersonic MiG-23 fighter bombers. This force sits just five miles from Japan's main northern island of Hokkaido.

Out of what was once little more than a coastal defense force, Moscow's Pacific Fleet now constitutes the single-largest component of the Soviet navy, consisting of 295 surface vessels, and 90 attack submarines, and 2,200 combat aircraft, including over 300 modern bombers and fighter bombers capable of striking any target in Japan or South Korea with nuclear weapons. The Soviet Far Eastern air force has been enhanced with assets capable of threatening the sea-lanes throughout the entire Western Pacific and Southeast Asia. Soviet missiles in Northeast Asia can now not only target objectives in North America but those as far south as the Philippines as well.

The Soviet navy treats the Sea of Okhotsk as a Soviet lake and seeks to dominate the Sea of Japan and the straits around the Japanese islands. Soviet military aircraft penetrate Japanese airspace almost daily. Moreover, Soviet forces have succeeded in gaining access to basing facilities in Southeast Asia that afford them immediate reach over those sea passages critical to the economic survival of Japan, the Republic of Korea and the Republic of China on Taiwan.

These military developments in East Asia constitute only part of a long-term program of Soviet aggressive expansion. Indeed, the Kremlin is determined that the Soviet Union shall become the dominant Asian power. In order to accomplish that, the USSR must neutralize Japan and the newly industrialized nations of Northeast Asia. It is also maneuvering to coopt and intimidate them economically and politically. One way of accomplishing this is to deploy its capabilities along vital supply routes that thread through the choke points located at the entrance and exit of the South China Sea. To effect its purpose, the Soviet Union has established what has become its largest out-of-area naval base at Cam Ranh Bay. This base now provides support for about thirty vessels, including conventional and nuclear-powered submarines and surface combatants, and the airfields in Vietnam provide facilities for fighter, bomber, and reconnaissance aircraft.

As noted elsewhere, the Soviets have undertaken the development of a new, all-weather port at Vostochny east of Vladivostok, have gained access to facilities at Najin, and are seeking additional facilities at Wonsan in southern North Korea. They are maneuvering to establish a broader presence throughout the Pacific, notably, as discussed below, in the southern Pacific islands.

Taken en masse, the simple threat of the ever-greater Soviet menace and expansion may be sufficient to intimidate America's allies and China into deference to the Soviet Union's arrogation of East Asian dominance, particularly if the USSR sought its protection payments in the form of economic and trade concessions. This would have a synergetic effect, facilitating the Soviet drive to develop Soviet Siberia. Moreover, it would force the burgeoning economies of East Asia to orient themselves away from the economic and political antipode of the United States and toward the military pole of the USSR. This would have a far-reaching ripple effect throughout the international economic and political order, enhancing Soviet influence and undermining that of the United States. The achievement of such a circumstance in itself would constitute no less a breakout, especially in the context of history, than the other possibilities discussed earlier.

UNDERMINING REGIONAL AND U.S. SECURITY

It is in this context of a possible Soviet breakout in East Asia that the U.S. military facilities in the Philippines have acquired increased strategic significance. For the first time since the end of World War II, a hostile military power threatens the security and integrity of the sea-lanes of Southeast Asia and the economic viability of the nations of Northeast Asia. As a consequence, the U.S. facilities at Subic Bay and Clark Air Field become essential to the maintenance of a credible deterrent posture in the Western Pacific.

Unfortunately, the future of the U.S. military facilities in the Philippines is clouded by uncertainties. Not only have a significant minority of Filipinos expressed objections to the presence of those facilities on Philippine soil, but an active communist insurgency on the islands threatens their security. Should the United States be required to evacuate the military facilities in the Philippine archipelago for whatever reason, the first consequence would be a major alteration in the balance of power throughout Asia to the decided advantage of the USSR. Not only would the economic, political, and strategic interests of the West suffer incalculable impairment, but the prospects for political democracy and economic well-being for the entire region would diminish drastically.

For all these reasons, the USSR has made the expulsion of the American military presence from the Philippines one of its highest priorities. Given the historic ties between the Philippines and the United States and the opportunities now presenting themselves in the Aquino era, the importance of this objective for the Soviet Union has dramatically increased in recent months. Success here would send shock waves throughout East Asia and the world. By itself, the loss to the United States of bases in the Philippines would inflict severe damage on

Western interests.   But the effect of the worst-case scenario—victory for the Soviet-backed communist rebels—would far outweigh the defeat of American interests in South Vietnam in 1975.   For the USSR, a communist victory in the Philippines would represent a breakout of the traditional kind.   On both the local and regional levels, it would rank with the consolidation of a communist government in Cuba.

The United States once relied upon the "containment line" of South Korea, Taiwan, and South Vietnam to meet such threats.   Obviously, this line no longer exists.   With the loss of the U.S. bases in Vietnam, followed by the voluntary abandonment of its facilities in Taiwan as an accommodation to Beijing, the only point left on this line is South Korea.   Given the present uncertainty over the future status of the Subic Bay and Clark bases in the Philippines, the "main defense line" connecting the latter with Okinawa and Japan could be effectively truncated at a critical point.   Not only would the loss of the Philippine bases jeopardize the defense of East Asia and the Pacific Basin, it would also severely affect the ability of the United States to project power into the highly volatile region of Southwest Asia and the Indian Ocean. This would also have serious ramifications for the security of the critical sea lines of communication connecting Europe and Asia.

While the ultimate defense line west of Hawaii—focusing on the present U.S. trust territories in the Pacific and Guam—remains intact, it is clearly unsuited by distance from Asia and lack of infrastructure for anything other than the actual forward defense of U.S. territory.   And even in this respect, there are emerging problems.

Most notably, the Soviet Union, directly and through proxies, is in the process of leapfrogging this line and establishing its own forward positions between it and Hawaii.   Thus, the Soviets have succeeded in obtaining a fishing rights agreement with Kiribati, which might afford the opportunity to lay the groundwork for naval facilities there.   In addition, as recently as May 6, 1986, the government of Vanuatu, which has refused to have diplomatic ties with either the United States or the USSR, announced that it planned to establish diplomatic links with Libya.   Prime Minister Walter Lini stated that he expected to receive Libyan aid once formal channels were opened.   It is also worth noting that Libyan meddling in French New Caledonia, to the north of Vanuatu, and Tripoli's support for the Kanak nationalists there may eventually lead to a Libyan/Soviet presence in that strategically located South Pacific island as well.

Given the current state of disarray in the Asia-Pacific theater, it is essential that Washington take the necessary steps to restructure its geostrategic posture in this vital region.   Toward this end, it must first stop the further erosion of its position and, at a minimum, reconfigure a credible containment line along the periphery of Asia. But discussion of the Soviet threat in East Asia requires an assessment of the risks now at hand in the region. Equally important is a thorough understanding of the parochial interests and anti-Soviet opportunities of the primary demographic presence in Asia, China; of the primary economic presence, Japan; and the Philippines.

THE PEOPLE'S REPUBLIC OF CHINA

Within the Asia-Pacific theater, the role of China has long been a matter of contention in U.S. national security circles. It is essential to the national security interests of the United States and its allies in the Free World that Washington's policies with regard to the People's Republic of China, which are inextricably linked to the security posture of the Republic of China on Taiwan, be based on realistic assumptions and considerations.

China is a regional power of growing importance, with an independent capacity to act as a force for stability in East Asia. On the other hand, it has also proven capable of belligerence: Chinese armed forces fought in Korea from 1950 to 1953, invaded Tibet in 1951 and completed its "liberation" in 1959, invaded India in 1962, seized the Paracel Islands in 1974, and invaded Vietnam in 1979. At the same time, in the context of the American-Soviet global confrontation, China represents a large buffer zone separating the two superpowers in much of the Asia-Pacific theater.

As a strategically located buffer, China becomes an important factor in balance-of-power calculations. Because China is in a position to block the projection of Soviet power into much of the Asia-Pacific theater, Soviet breakout strategy in Asia is designed in part to outflank mainland China. As a consequence, the Soviet Union, traditionally a land power, is striving to become a major sea power, with the bulk of its rapidly growing fleet now operating in the Pacific Ocean and adjacent waterways.

China as a Regional Power

From a geostrategic perspective, China poses nightmarish dilemmas for the Soviet Union. There is no serious prospect whatsoever that China will once again assume a position of subservience to Soviet leadership, as in the early Maoist period. The most that the Soviets might reasonably hope for would be an understanding between the two countries that would amount to a condominium in Asia, with China remaining neutral in any Soviet-American confrontation.

Starting in 1982, both the Soviet Union and China have actively sought normalization, and economic relations between the two have improved. However, this normalization process has not extended to matters of national security. With regard to the latter, Beijing has stipulated that three obstacles to normalization must be removed before there can be progress, and even then the relationship will be limited. Indeed, President Li Xiannian stipulated in July 1985:

> So long as the three obstacles are not removed, one can hardly think of normalizing Sino-Soviet relations. Even if the three obstacles are removed, the Sino-Soviet relationship will not revert to that of an alliance like the one in the 1950s. China is now determined to follow an independent course of diplomacy; it will not enter into an alliance with one power or another.

The three obstacles the Chinese want removed are nothing less than intrinsic elements of the Soviet strategy to achieve containment of China and facilitate an eventual Soviet breakout in the region:

1) Soviet support of Vietnam, which is critical to Vietnamese control of Cambodia as well as the rest of Indochina;
2) the stationing of large numbers of Soviet troops along the Sino-Soviet and Sino-Mongolian frontiers; and
3) the Soviet control and occupation of Afghanistan.

Soviet concern over the containment of China is largely rooted in the history of Sino-Russian relations over the last three centuries. The expansion of Russia across Asia beginning in the seventeenth century was accomplished in large measure at the expense of China, leading in the mid-nineteenth century to the imposition of a pattern of treaties and agreements that legitimated Russia's seizure of territories in Inner Mongolia, the Far East, and the Mongolian plateau.

Though the Ch'ing emperors, Manchus themselves, had been overlords of Manchuria, Inner and Outer Mongolia, Tibet, and a good part of Turkestan in Central Asia, their actual control of these lands was tenuous. The border regions then tended to be, and remain today, populated by a large percentage of non-Chinese peoples. By the end of the nineteenth century, through control of the Chinese Eastern Railway, the Russians were positioned to exercise hegemony over northern and central Manchuria. This was forestalled, however, by the Japanese victory in the Russo-Japanese War of 1904-5.

Although by agreement both Russia and Japan established spheres of influence in the province, Japan soon came to be the dominant power and in the 1930s transformed Manchuria into the puppet state of Manchukuo. In the meantime, China's influence in Outer Mongolia was also diminished as that province became the Mongolian People's Republic under Soviet protection in the 1920s. Japanese interest and influence in Inner Mongolia further weakened China's grip over the region of the Eastern Gobi. Another Chinese province, Xinjiang (Sinkiang), was virtually self-governing within the Soviet sphere of interest and under the effective control of the Soviet Red Army until that army was withdrawn after the outbreak of war in Eastern Europe.

The communist takeover in China portended a new era for the Russo-Chinese borderlands of Manchuria, Inner and Outer Mongolia, and Xinjiang. A new geopolitical environment seemed to have been created by the shared ideology between Moscow and Beijing, which suggested the emergence in the 1950s of a gigantic monolith spreading across Eurasia from East Berlin to Hanoi.

In the early 1960s, however, after the Sino-Soviet dispute had become a virtual cold war, it became evident that beneath the veneer of international communism lurked the conflicting demands of Russian and Chinese nationalism. It was learned that as early as 1954 Mao had approached Khrushchev and Marshal Nikolai Bulganin regarding the status of Outer Mongolia, and the Soviet leaders had refused to discuss the matter. That same year, *A Short History of Modern China* was published in Beijing and contained an illustration showing Outer Mongolia as an integral part of China and outlining those territories that had been lost by China more than a century earlier, including the Soviet Far East, the Pamirs, the Semirechiye, and the peninsulas of Southeast Asia.

In March 1963, for the first time, the *People's Daily* publicly aired the matter of China's territory losses to Russian imperialism in the nineteenth century. Its editorials indicated that China did not consider the status of any of these losses as beyond reconsideration and revision:

In the hundred years or so prior to the victory of the Chinese revolution, the imperialist and colonial powers—the United States, Britain, France, Tsarist Russia, Germany, Japan, Italy, Austria, Belgium, the Netherlands, Spain and Portugal—carried out unbridled aggression against China. They compelled the governments of old China to sign a large number of unequal treaties: the Treaty of Nanking in 1842, the Treaty of Aigun in 1858, the Treaty of Tientsin in 1858, the Treaty of Peking in 1860, the Treaty of Ili of 1881, the Protocol of Lisbon of 1887, the Treaty of Shimonoseki of 1895, the Convention for the Extension of Hong Kong of 1898, the Treaty of 1901, etc. By virtue of these unequal treaties, they annexed Chinese territory in the north, south, east and west and held leased territories on the seaboard and in the hinterland of China. . . .

At the time the People's Republic of China was inaugurated, our government declared that it would examine the treaties concluded by previous Chinese governments with foreign governments, treaties that have been left over by history, and would recognize, abrogate, revise or renegotiate them according to their respective contents. . . .

In September 1963, Beijing accused Moscow of subversion in Xinjiang, while the following month *Pravda* attacked the Chinese for "systematically violating the Soviet frontier" and illegally attempting to annex disputed territory at the confluence of the Ussuri and Amur rivers. In the fall of 1964, the Mongolian News Agency reported that

> the desire of the Chinese leaders to convert the Mongolian People's Republic into a province of China in effect does in no way differ from the predatory policy of the Chinese landlords and militarists, the Kuomintang reactionaries who are zealous opponents of the sovereignty of the Mongolian people. . . . The Chinese leaders' claims to Mongolia, whose history of statehood has roots in ancient times, are a result of the great power policy inherited from the Manchu-Chinese conquerors.

In the face of the failure of communist solidarity to override nationalism, the Soviets began incrementally to reinforce their military units along the Sino-Soviet border after 1960. By 1965, when Beijing began construction of an ICBM testing range, the Soviet Union had already begun to consider China as a potentially serious military threat.

In 1969, a serious border crisis developed that had long-lasting effects on Sino-Soviet relations. On March 2, Chinese forces ambushed and inflicted heavy casualties on a Soviet unit on Chen Pao (known to the Soviets as Damansky), a frozen island in the Ussuri River between the Soviet Maritime Province and Manchuria. On March 15, a Soviet force reciprocated in kind, overwhelming a Chinese force on the same island. On June 13, Moscow issued a virtual ultimatum demanding "consultations" with Beijing on the border problem within two or three months. On the date of the two-month deadline, August 13, Soviet troops occupied a hill two kilometers inside the Chinese border in western Xinjiang and defied the Chinese to force them out. The crisis was defused several weeks later when border negotiations began on October 20, 1969, talks that have continued periodically ever since without resolution of any of the fundamental matters at issue between the two countries.

At the same time, Moscow began to reinforce its conventional and nuclear forces along the Chinese border and in the Mongolian People's Republic. By 1973, Soviet strength near the Chinese border reached some fifty divisions, backed by substantial air power. Since then, Soviet power and military capability arrayed along the long frontier with China has reached awesome dimensions. However, despite this massive deployment, the Soviets still have much to worry about from China.

Of particular concern is the dramatic change in Chinese military doctrine that began to take shape about 1980. Chinese doctrine until then was fundamentally defensive. Its growing nuclear force was to serve as a strategic deterrent, while its huge people's militia stood ready to conduct massive guerrilla-war operations should China be attacked by conventional forces. The new doctrine that has since emerged calls for a strategic nuclear deterrent combined with a three-million-man, general-purpose, and modernized conventional army for use in nonnuclear warfare contingencies. The question that the Soviets must deal with is why China needs such a mobile, modern military force that would have such significant offensive capabilities. Edgar O'Ballance, writing in *Asian Defense Journal* (October 1985) suggests that

> While it is all very well to say that China will not have a credible expeditionary capability for another seven years or so, Gorbachev probably has a recurrent nightmare scenario about the pattern that Chinese military aggression might take against the Soviets in the future. . . .
>
> A widely spread out frontier war of attrition would disproportionately absorb Soviet military resources, and lead to a series of intermittent scuffles, rather than serious fighting. Chinese soldiers could forge forward in great numbers like ants in many different places simultaneously choosing points of penetration. In a struggle of this "eyeball-to-eyeball" nature, the Soviets may not be strong everywhere, nor be able to build an effective barrier along the whole length of this frontier. Therefore the Chinese could persistently and continually edge the Soviets backwards. . . .
>
> Having weakened, harassed and extended the Soviet armed forces in the Far East, the next Chinese move would be to gradually close in on them, sever the supporting railway lines, and subject them to a siege that would slowly tighten like a noose. Gorbachev then asks himself again, "Is it time to use nuclear weapons?" But still he is not sure. The Russians have never been lucky in their Far East wars (shades of 1904-5), and he would not want to risk the destruction of Soviet cities and the death of millions of Soviet citizens, simply to gain a respite in a war he knows he could not ultimately win, as the odds are on the much more populous Chinese nation. A nuclear attack, even from the tiny Chinese arsenal would cause death and destruction in the USSR on a sufficiently wide scale to make the price of a few square miles of Asian terrain far too Pyrrhic. Gorbachev wakes up in a cold sweat from his nightmare scenario to realise that one day he may have to fight and lose a conventional war against China.

While the Chinese threat may be mitigated in the near term through negotiations leading to accommodations, the long-term strategic dilemma remains. Also, there is the additional concern that any accommodation that would satisfy Chinese claims and demands would merely give them a needed respite to further strengthen their capability for confronting the Soviet Union militarily. One serious alternative open to the Soviets has been discussed by Edward N. Luttwak in *The Grand Strategy of the Soviet Union*:

At the level of grand strategy, any Soviet war scheme must start with two premises: that China is not destroyable, and that it cannot be occupied in its totality to be remade to order. . . . This leaves only one feasible goal for a Soviet war: if an independent China of growing power can be neither tolerated nor destroyed, then it must be divided. What Soviet military power can achieve directly is the conquest of territories which can be turned into client states; obviously, this is feasible only where the population includes a large non-Chinese element.

This suggests that a Soviet threat to carve up China would focus primarily on the thinly populated and ethnically mixed regions of Xinjiang, Tibet, Qinghai, northern Gansu, Inner Mongolia, and the northern part of Heilongjiang in northern Manchuria. These provinces and regions comprise about fifty-six percent of China's territory but only six percent of the population, a third of which is non-Chinese.

All in all, China as a regional power thus presents a geostrategic dilemma of the highest order for the Soviet Union and a security threat that cannot be ignored. These problems are compounded significantly when China is considered as a possible buffer zone in the Soviet-American confrontation in the Asia-Pacific theater.

U.S. COUNTERVAILING STRATEGY

The problems of the U.S. strategy in the Asia-Pacific arena have grown over the past decade in an almost direct relationship to the increase in importance of the region. The removal of U.S. forces from the strategically located and intact naval and air bases in Vietnam, followed by the withdrawal of U.S. air forces from Thailand, have created major impediments to effective power projection in the vast area along Asia's southern periphery from the Persian Gulf to the South China Sea. These problems are further compounded by the Soviets' accession of the bases in Vietnam, which give Moscow an unprecedented capability for the projection of its own power in Southeast Asia, in addition to that of its local ally.

The security of U.S. interests in the Western Pacific is indivisible from the security of its trading partners from Japan to Australia. Hence the primary U.S. strategic aim in the region must be to prevent the Soviet Union from achieving effective hegemony in Asia and its environs either by the Soviets' unopposed actual projection of power or through the more subtle process of preemptive intimidation based on the presumption of their overwhelming power-projection capabilities. Being a maritime power, the United States must therefore pursue its strategic aims through a series of forward defense lines that traverse the vast distance between the United States and the Soviet Union. These lines not only constitute the basis for power projection westward toward Asia but also provide strategic depth in a defensive posture against Soviet power projection eastward from Asia.

As suggested by General Wego W.K. Chiang in *The Strategic Significance of Taiwan,* there are essentially five such defense lines between the United States and the Soviet Union in the Asia-Pacific theater. In terms of proximity to the United States, the ultimate line of defense west of the Hawaiian Islands lies in a chain of widely dispersed points roughly between 135 degrees and 145 degrees longitude east of Greenwich and stretching from Japan to the Mariana Islands, Guam, and the Caroline Islands. Further west lies what is sometimes characterized as the "main defense line" connecting Japan, the Ryukyu Islands, and the Philippines. Still closer to the Asian mainland lies the containment line from South Korea to Taiwan that once reached to Indochina. A fourth forward line, on the mainland, would run from Beijing to Lanzhou to Tibet. The fifth and most advanced line of defense would stretch along the present Sino-Soviet frontier from Heilongjiang through Inner Mongolia to Xinjiang. The problems of U.S. strategy can be brought into sharp relief by an examination of these layered lines of defense in the Asia-Pacific theater.

Ideally, the best place to block Soviet power projection is at its source, that is, at the Sino-Soviet border. Were Washington and Beijing to join in a mutual defense pact, the very notion of Soviet hegemonic ambitions in the Pacific Basin would become idle. Indeed, such a defense alliance would alter dramatically the geopolitical and geostrategic environment in Asia. Thus, President Ronald Reagan, in his accompanying statement on the joint U.S.-PRC communiqué on arms sales to Taiwan on August 17, 1982, stated:

> Building a strong and lasting relationship with China . . . is vital to our long-term national security interests and contributes to stability in East Asia. It is in the national interest of the United States that this important strategic relationship be advanced.

However, there is good reason to believe that a viable alliance built on this "strategic relationship" is inconceivable in the foreseeable future, except possibly at such time when it would have already lost its potential as a deterrent to further Soviet adventurism in Asia. In late December 1983, the director of Beijing's Institute for International Affairs, Huan Xian, noted:

> Near the end of the Carter Administration's term and at the beginning of the term of the Reagan Administration, the Americans determinedly and energetically put up a front against the Soviet Union politically and militarily in the struggle for superiority in

nuclear armament, in the matter of the European intermediate-range weapons, in the
Caribbean region, in the Middle East and finally, also in Asia.

This stopped the Soviet Union, and the rivalry of the two superpowers considerably
intensified throughout the world. It seems that the Russians still do not feel strong
enough to react to the U.S. offensive. In our view, a certain balance between the two
has emerged, especially in the military field.

It would appear then, from Beijing's perspective, that China has already reaped an improved security posture as a consequence of stronger
U.S. national security policy over the last decade and has little interest
in disturbing this *perceived* balance between the two superpowers. In
the absence of a Beijing-Washington entente, the forward defense line
along the Sino-Soviet frontier loses all strategic significance for both
the United States and China. Since, from the perspective of China as a
regional power, this line is basically indefensible, China itself must think
of the Beijing-Lanzhou-Tibet line as its own best option for defense
against a Soviet threat to dismember the country.

One can imagine that, in the event of a Soviet attempt to carve
China into more manageable pieces, Beijing might well seek a military
alliance with Washington that would help stop the Soviet advance at the
Beijing-Lanzhou-Tibet line. There are, however, no signs that Beijing is
interested in such a relationship now, notwithstanding the tangible
evidence of Washington's continuing contributions to the development of
Beijing's military potential. Furthermore, in such a situation, significant
levels of intra-communist contact would exist that the Chinese might
activate to defuse the Soviet threat.

In this regard, the evolving Washington-Beijing relationship must be
tempered by strategic realism. While it serves U.S. security interests to
improve China's military potential as a regional land power, thus enhancing its credibility as a potential threat to the Soviet Union and its con-
tinental allies (Vietnam and Mongolia), it does not serve U.S. interests
to assist China in developing an extracontinental power-projection
capability.

Furthermore, given the uncertainty of China's position in the event
of heightened tension in the region between the United States and the
Soviet Union—whether with respect to a crisis in the Korean peninsula,
along the Thai-Kampuchean-Laotian frontier, or in Southwest Asia—the
United States must view with concern any expansion of Beijing's capacity to exercise control over the critical sea lines of communication tra-
versing the seas between Japan and the Indian Ocean. Since the possibility of a Sino-Soviet rapprochement cannot be foreclosed, should it
prove expedient, the United States must give more serious consideration
to the strategic implications of any move by Beijing to coerce Taipei

into a reunification of Taiwan with mainland China under its present regime.

Furthermore, the security of the sea-lanes should not be mortgaged for the expectation of improved commercial relations with mainland China. China (Beijing) should not be viewed as a tradeoff for China (Taipei), even though the former prefers to see its relations with the United States in such a manner. Clearly, both are important to America's own national security interests. It would constitute strategic folly to jeopardize the autonomy of Taiwan. While there is considerable doubt about what Beijing would do about a Soviet threat to Western Pacific security, there is none whatsoever about Taiwan's readiness to commit itself to the defense of Free World interests in the region. (This assumes but a modicum of Taiwanese confidence in the U.S. commitment to its survival and independence.) Indeed, Taiwan, strategically located at the juncture of the East China and South China seas, should be properly perceived as a critical center point in a new containment line reaching from South Korea and Japan to the Philippines.

THE NEW ECONOMIC POWER: JAPAN

The very success that Japan has achieved now calls into question the posture it has maintained in its defense and security policies. As an emerging world economic power and political leader, Japan can no longer remain a silent and passive partner in the alliance that formally guarantees its own security. Nor can it remain indifferent to the increasingly threatening posture of the USSR in the seas around Japan, as detailed above.

As Article IX of Japan's postwar constitution asserts, ". . . the Japanese people forever renounce war as a sovereign right of the nation, and the threat or use of force as a means of settling international disputes . . . land, sea and air forces, as well as other war potential, will never be maintained. The right of belligerency of the state will not be recognized." This renunciation of militarism has become fixed in the Japanese political psyche. For example, as of March 1986, Japan's combined Ground, Air and Maritime Self-Defense Forces totalled 245,421 troops, 9.8 percent below their budgeted strength of 272,162. Japan's current military force levels thus are exceeded by every country in East Asia, except the Philippines.

Writing in the Winter 1987 issue of *Global Affairs*, Professor Klaus H. Pringsheim stated:

Japan's security policy remains exclusively defensive in nature. Accordingly, Japan may not possess weapons systems that are offensive in nature, such as ICBMs and long-range strategic bombers, nor can it dispatch forces bearing arms abroad, since such deployment would go beyond the minimum necessary for self-defense. Japan, moreover, has committed itself not to institute military conscription. Another self-imposed restriction affecting Japan's defense capabilities is the 1 percent of gross national product (GNP) ceiling on Japan's defense expenditures first instituted by Prime Minister Takeo Miki in 1976. This ceiling was instituted in response to opposition charges that the defense budgetary policies of the LDP would take Japan down the road to the resurgence of militarism and aggression. . . .

Adherence to this self-imposed ceiling has put Japan in a class by itself at the low end of military expenditures among major nations of the world. By comparison, the United States spends 7.2 percent (of GNP), the Soviet Union as much as 15 percent (est.), West Germany 4.3 percent, the United Kingdom 5.1 percent, France 4.1 percent, Italy 2.6 percent, Canada 2 percent, Israel 37.9 percent, South Korea 7.6 percent, Taiwan 7.3 percent and even Switzerland 2.1 percent. Among all these countries Japan is lowest not only in percentage of GNP expenditure for defense, but in per capita expenditure and percentage of general account budget expenditure as well.

As noted earlier in this chapter, the USSR has placed ground, air, and naval forces near Japan far in excess of any conceivable threat. Realistically, Japan has three tasks that it might accomplish militarily in the near future that have been the subject of discussion between successive Japanese and American administrations:

1) to protect and monitor the sea-lanes around Japan to a distance of one-thousand miles from the main island of Honshu in cooperation with the U.S. Seventh Fleet;
2) to provide an air-defense screen across the Japanese archipelago with the electronic monitoring of Soviet air and naval activity, particularly of long-range bomber, fighter, and tactical aircraft; and
3) to develop the capacity to block the four vital straits that give access to or provide exits from the Sea of Japan, where two major Soviet naval bases—Vladivostok and Sovietskaya Gavan—are located: the Korea Strait, Tsushima Strait, Tsugaru Strait, and La Perouse Strait (Soya Kaikyo). As Pringsheim emphasizes,

if Japan's Maritime Self Defense Forces, in collaboration with the U.S. Seventh Fleet, can accomplish this, it will effectively bottle up the Soviet Far Eastern Fleet in the Sea of Japan and severely hamper its ability to disrupt Japan's vital sea lanes to the south, as well as cut off the Soviet supply lines to Cam Ranh Bay, Danang and the Indian Ocean.

Accomplishing this, Pringsheim notes, would require Japan's having to spend about 2.5 percent of GNP for defense and the purchase of new military equipment, including destroyers, submarines, antisubmarine warfare (ASW) aircraft, and fighter/interceptors to meet the USSR's naval-attached Backfire bombers.

In this context, Soviet policy toward Japan has aimed at four objectives, as characterized by Pringsheim:

1) To dampen the enthusiasm for a substantial beefing up of Japan's Self Defense Forces that Soviet "Backfire Diplomacy" has aroused; 2) to loosen the military, ideological and economic ties between the United States and Japan; 3) to obtain substantial Japanese investment and technology transfers, particularly to the Soviet Far East, to strengthen both the economic and military infrastructure in that area; and 4) to forestall the possible emergence of a quasi-regional alliance among the United States, Japan, South Korea, Taiwan, and, in the long run, even China and the ASEAN nations against the further expansion of Soviet influence in Northeast, Southeast and South Asia.

Ideally, then Moscow would like to turn Japan into an unarmed neutral country deferential to the USSR's global geopolitical ambitions. The ultimate aims of a Soviet breakout toward Japan would include the following:

- to orient Japan away from the West, economically and politically;
- to intimidate or persuade Japan into organizing, underwriting, and financing Soviet development in Eastern Siberia;
- to assure that Japan will supply machinery and technology to bolster the sagging Soviet economy;
- to transform Japan into an even wider conduit of high-technology goods and information from the West to the USSR;
- to make Japan consume more Soviet raw materials, purchase more Soviet goods and processes, and act as a marketing agent and market force for the Soviet Union in the world economy;
- to forestall Japanese remilitarization;
- to utilize Japan as an economic, political, and military counterbalance against a renascent China;
- to isolate Japan from its democratic allies and intimidate it into forswearing any regional role; and
- to manipulate Japan so that it undermines America's political interests, economic position, and security objectives.

Despite Japan's great economic strength and sophisticated industrial capacity, its lack of adequate defenses against the growing power of the USSR encourages Moscow to apply more pressure on Tokyo. For example, the Soviet Union would like to menace Japan with nuclear weapons scant miles from its shores, to threaten terrible retribution if

Japan participates in the Strategic Defense Initiative, and to force on Japan unbalanced agreements on a host of other matters affecting Japan's national interest. As an economic superpower, however, Japan must recognize that it cannot relinquish its inherent responsibility of self-defense. Japan's understandable concern with its interpretation of constitutional constraints on its self-defense forces must be balanced with a commitment to protect its people against intimidation and threat of attack. This is especially true in light of the fact that Soviet activities in East Asia have been increasing and that Soviet adventurism in the region is expanding its reach.

It is obvious that Japan must do more to protect its coasts, straits, sea-lanes, and airspace from Soviet domination. This requires a substantial increase in Japan's direct defense spending. Perhaps even more important, Japan can and should do more to provide for Asian security *by contributing to the support of other military forces in the area*. This latter approach is one that has not been utilized in the past. Despite the permanence of Japan's resistance to what it regards as militarism and given its great wealth and increasing economic and political responsibilities in the region, Japan can materially enhance its own security and that of its democratic partners by underwriting more of the defense efforts that they themselves mount.

South Korea, Taiwan, the Philippines, Thailand, and Australia are all likely candidates for Japanese subventions of their military outlays. This would facilitate an actual *expansion* of the capabilities of the West against Soviet expansion and intimidation. Japan would benefit both directly, through increased regional security, and indirectly, through a decrease in the USSR's ability to threaten and coerce Japan and its allies. By encouraging Japan to assume a greater responsibility for its own defense and by taking into account the particular strengths and weaknesses of each nation comprising the de facto democratic Asian alliance, the United States can facilitate an effective response to the Soviet threat and prevent a breakout designed to shatter, demoralize, and parasitize the economic and political structure of democratic Asia.

Given this, the proper approach to the Philippines becomes clearer: Japan, South Korea, Taiwan, and the Philippines, acting in concert with a reconstituted U.S. security position in the region, offer the brightest prospect for assuring the continued growth and stability that has made the Western Pacific Basin the envy of the world and most particularly of the Soviet Union and its allies. Enhanced political unity and stability and sustained economic growth in the Philippines would reduce the recruitment potential and sustainability of its communist and secessionist insurgencies. The United States and its allies, particularly Japan, should expand trade opportunities and aid for the Philippines and contribute economic and/or military aid to foster stability and growth.

There is every reason to believe that with stability and growth the government of the Philippines would be disposed to support the continued presence of U.S. military facilities in the Philippines. Without that stability and growth, the prospects increase that anti-American elements would exploit the general distress not only to the disservice of the United States but at the ultimate expense of Philippine interests as well. The kinds of economic and military support required by the Republic of the Philippines should be made available in sufficient quantities and in a manner that would not impair the sovereign integrity of a respected security partner.

The new government of the Philippines must recognize, in its own interest in survival as a vibrant democracy in a traditionally authoritarian part of the world, that its security is bound up with the security posture of the United States in the Asia-Pacific theater. It should be urged to dispel any lingering concern about its commitment to the security of the South China Sea region in the context of a broader, multilateral defensive coalition based on the backbone of a strong U.S. military presence. A concerted American policy here, amplified by a redoubled Japanese political and, especially, economic commitment, will ultimately prove persuasive and stabilizing not only for the Philippines but for the region as a whole.

CHAPTER 9
Shortcomings in American Strategy-Making

The United States must develop and implement an effective and consistent counterstrategy, able to meet an ever-evolving Soviet threat. If the United States fails to do this, the world will end up with one predominant superpower capable of permanently milking the industrial democracies to sustain its unreformed totalitarian system and its aggressive foreign appetites. Like a great bully, the Soviet Union's unchallenged military power and the ever-increasing credibility of its intimidating demeanor will put the Western democracies into an economic, political, and military lock. This will produce a kind of reverse mercantilism, one that saps the West economically, ideologically, and spiritually. Ultimately, these tactics can only prove more threatening and dreadful than the use of nuclear weapons.

DETERMINANTS OF U.S. POLICY

To think strategically, a policy planner must accept and not be ashamed of the power of his nation. He must be willing to articulate a clear definition of national interests and to participate in the maintenance of the consensus about those national interests. The strategists must be willing to assign priorities to regions and issues, ranking them accordingly. He must define the passage of time in ways that may separate events and results from the policy planners initially involved in them. He must have a worldview, deciding upon what kind of a world he truly aspires to create and realistically believes can be achieved. He must speak in nouns, not adjectives; that is, he must do more than favor a "democratic" world, a "free" world, a "peaceful" world. He must define in practical terms where he expects the nation, its allies, its clients, and its adversaries to be years and decades down the road. And he must always be open to creative and alternative means to achieve the strategic goals he and other strategists in U.S. policy organizations have helped set for the nation.

But unlike its adversaries, the United States lacks any true strategy-making institution with effective policy planners. There is no analogue of the Clausewitzian *Gross Generalstab*, a group of experts dedicated to considering the position and interests of the state decades down the road and the way in which these future interests and objectives might be promoted, achieved, and defended. Various aspects of the Soviet problem are regularly discussed by many individuals in the U.S. government such as intelligence officials who derive National Intelligence Estimates, State Department experts in the Bureau of Soviet Affairs, and Pentagon officials attached to the various military intelligence agencies, the staff of the Joint Chiefs, and various strategic policy and doctrine offices. The United States certainly has a large number of contingency war plans and a Strategic Integrated Operating Plan to manage a range of hostile interactions with the USSR. Yet nearly all that passes for strategy in the United States is, in fact, battle strategy, or the coordinated integration of (primarily military) tactics. It is taken as an unchallenged assumption in the United States that a grand strategy is inherently spelled out in the very nature of the American system. Americans naively believe political democracy, democratic capitalism, consumerism, toleration, and opportunity are the natural aspirations of humankind, and given the chance, most people will naturally gravitate to this state of affairs.

Indeed, this argument has considerable merit. It is certainly true that most people living under situations of political and social oppression naturally desire to implement various aspects of the American model if the opportunity (the breakdown of local autocracy) arises. Yet the American model is not universally appealing, as any brief acquaintance with modern Islamic societies (and not just that of Iran) can demonstrate. Moreover, history has repeatedly shown that the mere possession of a superior moral, spiritual, and political system is no guarantee of the survival of that system or of the broader interests of the nation that possesses that system. These factors are especially relevant when considering the Soviet threat, since the United States confronts not only a military adversary but an ideological one as well. Though the Soviet salient is a function of Russian power and control (not Marxist-Leninist social justice, as the Soviets claim), it is mediated and advanced by an ideological dialectic designed to discredit Western democratic values. It is no longer sufficient to hold truths about democracy to be self-evident, nor can it be assumed that once the West recognizes the strategic Soviet threat (if indeed it does) it will take action to thwart it.

There has never been a serious national debate in the United States on strategy. Even the new concepts of no-first-use, nuclear freeze, and SDI emerged with only minimal discussion within the administrations that initiated them. Perhaps it is impossible for democracies to plan for the long term, since leaders respond to local, parochial issues and short-term concerns. Can a democracy evolve a coherent, long-term strategy in its confrontation with a totalitarian power? Professor Richard Pipes believes apparently not. A democracy can do it on a short-term basis in wartime, he observes, as was demonstrated during World War II, but developing an effective strategy during a twilight period—during an indeterminate era of no peace, no war—represents a much greater challenge to a government's national security institutions.

Strategy-making entails a number of operating assumptions. Yet consider how complex this task can become when one describes the strategic process in the most simple terms: "We are here now. We want to get there. How do we do it?" The first sentence assumes that a consensus can be reached about the fundamental geostrategic position of the United States. This assessment requires not just a sense of positioning but also of momentum: Is our geostrategic position improving? Or weakening? What constitutes an "improvement"? What constitutes "weakening"? To say "We want to get there" also assumes that some consensus can be reached about what should constitute the goals and objectives of the United States over time on both a macro and micro scales, and by a number of military, political, economic, and ideological standards.

"How do we do it?" requires a third consensus on means to specific ends. It also implies that the means agreed upon will be followed consistently over the life of many Congresses and several presidential administrations. Yet exigencies arise, and then the following question must be confronted: How do we agree that a challenge has arisen that requires a change in course? How do we agree on when a change in course is necessary? How do we agree on the means with which to meet the new challenge? How do we then implement them?

OBSTACLES TO EFFECTIVE PLANNING

Avoiding Specifics

The United States is a market economy in both an economic and a political sense. The United States has always eschewed centralized planning in economics with the understanding that given reasonable protection and stability the forces of the market and the vitality of experimentation inherent in a modified laissez-faire economy would generate an efficient means of meeting the needs of the marketplace. Similarly, in the realm of international strategy, the United States has eschewed specific, grand strategies. Instead, our preferred method has been to promote general principles of economic and social freedom and use our power to protect the continued right to choose. Thus far, this approach has been congenial to the American democratic spirit since it has reflected a number of national physical and intellectual characteristics:

- the insulation afforded by the oceans;
- the lack of threats from either north or south;
- the distaste, articulated by America's founders, for the Byzantine maneuverings of Old World politics; and
- a similar discomfort with entangling alliances.

The entire concept of a state power with state objectives and a regard for the balance of power was alien to the American outlook. To be sure, throughout our history there have been outstanding examples of long-range, American strategies such as the Monroe Doctrine, the Open Door Policy on China, the Marshall Plan, and the formation of NATO. But these are outstanding in part because they are so much at variance with the norm of American planning in the international sphere.

Politicking for Short-term Gains

The American approach always has been shaped by political realities. Periodic power shifts are institutionally programmed into the workings of American government to assure that those in power will be more responsive to the electorate and to other centers of power. While this approach is often inefficient, it is an accepted part of the price the American people pay for insurance that our democracy will not degenerate into oligarchy and autocracy, even for the best of reasons.

But this political reality challenges those who would make strategy. If one is really trying to think strategically, one cannot think in two-year or four-year increments. Moreover, we are not a nation of chess players or Go players, thinking in terms of effects many stages hence; we tend to think quickly in terms of a never-ending series of crises. Decision-makers understand that instituted policy plans have to produce tangible results in at most a four-year cycle. If not, there is an institutional and psychological resistance to coming up with the financial and political investments necessary to sustain the policy.

The lack of long-term planning is not merely confined to strategic thinkers; it is also a characteristic of American business (and the fact that many executives from the business world fill crucial positions in each administration is not irrelevant here.) Institutions such as insurance companies and pension plans, have come to be dominant stockholders in major corporations and have come to expect rapid, short-term financial results. This lack of investment undermines long-term business planning and is one of the reasons Japanese firms have been able to sustain decade-long efforts to win a percentage of American markets.

Analogously, politicians find themselves facing short-term institutional pressures from the ballot-box standards by which they assume public opinion will validate their successes and punish their failures. The process feeds on itself as pressure mounts within the system for regular foreign policy spectaculars of no real substance and against long-term capital investments without prospects of immediate payoffs, political, strategic, or otherwise. Part of this owes to the nature of American electoral politics, to aspects of the American psyche, and to personnel policies that assume a steady and relatively rapid turnover and/or rotation in nearly all positions in government, the military, and the intelligence services. A senior American official who holds the same post for eight years is not only an anomaly but his peers often consider him to be lacking in ambition. In contrast, many Eastern Bloc officials, especially those in the military and the intelligence services, have tenures measured in decades.

Each approach has obvious advantages and shortcomings. But one advantage that long tenure gives the Eastern Bloc is the ability to make long-term investments in political strategies and human assets without having to worry about a payoff for years or even decades. Furthermore, it enables the Eastern Bloc to make better use of those resources that promote strategy. Less specifically task oriented, these resources can be employed with greater flexibility. And the surety of tenure means that strategic managers can seize opportunities as they arise or wait patiently without having to worry too much about seeking short-term "victories" that validate their bureaucratic raison d'être.

The mounting of an effective strategy requires long-term investments and a willingness to sustain those investments even when there is seemingly little need for them and when a budget cut is politically attractive. A textbook example of this was the cutback in the training of Farsi speakers sanctioned by the U.S. government in the 1970s. The assumption was that there was no pressing need to maintain this cadre of linguists, given Iran's alignment with the United States. Yet two implicit assumptions were fundamentally faulty here: first, that trustworthy Farsi speakers could somehow be acquired if suddenly needed, and second, that Iran would remain aligned with the United States.

Strategy-making, therefore, requires a certain cold-blooded testing of assumptions for the national interest. In the case of Iran, it is clear that in a variety of policy areas, there was strong political pressure not to interfere in the shah's shaky situation or to explore potential alternatives and their implications, for fear of giving offense to this crucial client. Yet this left the United States unprepared both strategically and tactically to cope with the Islamic Revolution and its aftermath. Worse, it allowed already untested strategic assumptions about the underlying community of interests between the United States and Iran to continue in place unchallenged *after* the shah was overthrown. This inevitably set the stage for American policy defeats in the embassy-hostage crisis and the Iranian arms deal.

The nearest the United States comes to true strategic planning is in the field of nuclear weapons, which requires a commitment of money and policy over the life of several administrations and is assumed fundamentally and permanently to change the nature of U.S.-Soviet relations. The Strategic Defense Initiative stands out for the strategic vision underlying its conception. SDI is not simply a weapon; in its essence it is a politico-military initiative designed to

1) invalidate the immense investment the Soviets have made in their strategic rocket forces and thus
2) place massive strains upon the Soviet economy and Soviet leadership, in turn
3) eliciting a more compliant, less aggressive Soviet attitude across the board.

Yet the Reagan administration has refused to educate the American people, the Congress, and our allies to this fundamental reality of SDI's worth. (It is not something the Soviets do not understand, nor is it something for which we should be ashamed.) The administration has presented SDI as something that is in the interest of the Soviets (it is not) and that could be shared (it could not). In a sense, the Reagan administration, fearful of appearing too strategically intent, has refused to utilize the strongest arguments of all, those of geopolitical strategy. The net result of publicly ignoring SDI's strategic implications has called into question its entire validity, defined the debate as simply one more about the efficacy of a weapon system, and slowed the momentum toward the development and emplacement of SDI. Interestingly, the terrestrial application of one particular SDI technology, electromagnetic rail guns, would similarly invalidate the gigantic investment the USSR has made in its conventional armored forces. Deployed along with SDI, it would have a profoundly inhibiting effect on Soviet aggressiveness. Yet the United States has not moved energetically enough to demonstrate the utility of the concept or to defend the strategic validity of implementing it.

SDI is a tremendous asset to the United States, but it should not be forgotten that the strategic aspect of SDI is as a weapon strategy. Such things are certainly useful (weapons have geopolitical effects, after all), but they tend to be transient and can be neutralized or circumvented, as the history of warfare demonstrates. A good tactic may be tantamount to a strategy, but it is no substitute for a broader, integrated geopolitical plan that utilizes technical innovations simply as *part* of a larger set of means and objectives.

As of now, the strategic confrontation between the two superpowers continues to be determined by the Soviets, ceding to them the advantage of choosing the setting wherein each scene on the global stage will be played out. Unless dealings with the Soviets are conducted with reference to a set of clear U.S. goals that transcend the merely reactive, the United States cannot but cede to the Soviets the option of attacking the status quo at their pleasure. We must not permit the Kremlin to remain in the position of *setting our priorities* by forcing a reaction to its initiatives. To overcome this, the United States must first overcome a variety of functional shortcomings in its strategic operations, such as they are.

THE TRAP OF ARMS CONTROL: TACTICS AS STRATEGY

Since the advent of the era of détente, the United States has made the pursuit of strategic arms agreements the centerpiece of American "strategy" toward the USSR. But there are a number of problems with this approach. First, the effect of strategic arms agreements on worldwide Soviet adventurism is limited. Soviet activities in Angola, Ethiopia, Libya, and South Yemen perceptibly accelerated after the Nixon-Brezhnev summits. The Soviets egged on the Organization of Petroleum Exporting Countries' (OPEC) oil boycott and OPEC's subsequent oil-pricing aggression and actively aided the Arab attack on Israel during the 1973 October War.

Second, strategic arms agreements, at best, have only affected the strategic arms balance. Mostly, they have not even had that effect. These agreements certainly have not moved the superpowers toward a fundamentally different era of peace and accommodation. The superpower dialectic takes place on a number of levels and in a number of currencies—economic, political, social, and military. American policymakers consistently have expressed the *hope* that strategic arms agreements would lead to a broader dialogue between the superpowers, culminating in a change in the strategic climate beneficial to the cause of freedom and openness. But the Soviets have always restricted the long-term, substantive impact of strategic arms agreements to the military sphere. They certainly have not been above using the diplomacy of strategic arms negotiations to promote their own political interests and image. But they have not stopped defining this in terms of a correlation of forces increasingly favorable to the USSR and increasingly harmful to the United States.

Moreover, while the Soviets have favored strategic arms limitations agreements that have a long-term, substantive impact in the military sphere, they have defined that impact in a way inimical to American assumptions. The Soviets believe arms control agreements should slow or eliminate American advantages in weapon development and deployment and should facilitate or solidify Soviet advantages. Soviet behavior since the ratification of the ABM Treaty and the negotiation of the SALT II Treaty exemplifies this attitude.

Finally, the pursuit of strategic arms limitation treaties can become an end in itself and highly politicized as well. As President Reagan has demonstrated with the INF Treaty, an administration—especially one in need of a public relations triumph to boost its sagging image—may agree to an ill-conceived, unequal treaty. It may also suspend larger strategic thinking and policy implementation so as not to endanger the public relations show associated with summitry and the treaty signing.

THE PEACE DEFINITION TRAP

The preoccupation of American policymakers with their public image is inextricably tied to the American failure to grasp the nature of peace and the nature of war. We tend to see them in opposition to each other. We do not see the use of force or the threat of force as an intrinsic part of the peace process, or the correlation between power and diplomacy, or that one has peace as long as one has a credible threat. Americans see peace as friendship, such as we enjoy with Canada. So the natural American reflex when confronted with the possibility of peace is a move toward disarmament. In reality, true peace in the nuclear age resembles, at best, a working, permanent armistice. To think otherwise is to fall into the Soviet trap, accepting the argument that such things as SDI and missiles are not necessary if peace is achieved and, indeed, should be discarded up front as a sign of good intentions.

Problems with the definition of peace are born of an innate if somewhat naïve American desire for good neighborliness and honesty. In matters of strategy, the effect of this attitude has been seen repeatedly since the beginning of the Cold War. Americans find it difficult to stick to a long-term strategy with the fundamental assumption the fact that true peace is not achievable. Appreciating this, the Soviets have periodically initiated peace overtures with one purpose in mind: to derail the achievement of a strategic consensus within the United States about the implacable nature of the Soviet threat (and ineluctably, about the necessity of implementing a long-term, consistent strategy to meet that threat).

PERCEPTUAL DISUNITY

Sometimes the Free World wins a particular skirmish (Grenada, for example) or holds off conquest with surprising firmness (Afghanistan, for example). But such Free World "victories" are not cumulative, precisely because they are not perceived as fitting within the frame of a global design, or even as specific *Free World* victories at all.

The Soviets' most valuable ally in this war is Western disunity, beginning with *the disunity of fundamental understanding*. So, with a flexible timetable, the Soviets can adjust their global design as necessary, cut losses as their priorities dictate, and move forward relentlessly on all remaining fronts or open new ones. Throughout this process, they can foment divisions among the Western allies about the true nature of Soviet intentions and about the best tactic to defuse further, "justified" Soviet defense of its "legitimate interests."

Part of America's problem, as noted by Richard Pipes, is an overcompartmentalization of the world and its conflicts. Policymakers must look at each threat and the responding strategy in global terms; they must correlate how local challenges by the Soviet Union can impact upon both the nuclear balance and the overall geopolitical balance. Soviet strategy is global; *Western strategists must look at the facets of the strategy and synthesize the overall threat*. They must look at each arena and judge how this relates to *other* Soviet options and opportunities, fully elucidating the functionally integrated, world reach of Soviet strategy.

As noted earlier, the United States tends to look at conflicts as if their implications and costs were confined to one region. But a defeat in Central America or southern Africa, for instance, can have a measurable, deleterious effect on American policy in other regions. It is certain to encourage the Soviets to employ similar tactics elsewhere. The Soviets' operating assumption is that having succeeded in one region with a particular technique, they and their clients may have found an approach that attacks a systemic weakness of the West and may be applicable in other areas. It may even elicit the same, unproductive, even counterproductive American response.

The Soviets think in terms of processes. They naturally view American failures in terms of the weak American strategic processes thus illuminated. Given this, the Soviet Union is apt to challenge the United States in a number of areas with similar tactics until it becomes clear that overall American strategizing has changed and not just local theater tactics. This pattern was apparent during the 1970s, when similar tactics were used in Angola, Ethiopia, and finally Afghanistan. A similar attempt was made in the early 1980s, when the lessons of revolutionary Cuba were tried first in Nicaragua, then El Salvador.

FAILURE TO RECOGNIZE CONNECTIVITY

The strategic battle is fought and facilitated at the local, conventional level. The overcompartmentalization mentioned previously is not only a horizontal but a vertical phenomenon. American policymakers too often operate as if the U.S.-Soviet competition were only played out in the dealings between the superpowers themselves and only through the true "statesmen's issues," such as arms control, détente, and regional peacemaking.

As Pipes has pointed out, the Soviet view of warfare does not differentiate between the magnitude of the weapons used and the size of the combatants involved. Americans categorize warfare by local, theater conventional, theater nuclear, and strategic nuclear. But the Soviets categorize by the Marxist, dialectical nature of the conflict, calling them wars of imperialism, anticolonialist wars, bourgeois revolutions, peoples' revolutions led by a revolutionary avant-garde, wars in defense of the gains of socialism, wars to implement the momentum of history through the expansion of the workers' states, etc.

It is beyond question that the Soviets view their dialectical, "peaceful" dealings with the West in a similar fashion. The USSR does not differentiate between events that have an effect on relations between the superpowers and those that do not. Certainly, they appreciate that many policy initiatives are primarily local in nature. But they never assume that these initiatives are purely local, or that they lack Marxist dialectical content, or that the cumulative, collective effect of these small but ideologically proper policies will not eventually be felt on the largest stage, where the conflict between socialism and capitalist imperialism is played out for keeps.

The Soviets operate on the assumption that successes in such high-level fields as nuclear weapons pave the way for successes on the local level, and local breakthroughs can strengthen the Soviet position versus the United States. A moment's reflection demonstrates the truth of this: The Soviet nuclear buildup makes local power projection by the USSR and its clients in such disparate places as Afghanistan, Angola, and the Philippines much more credible. Conversely, local Western reverses, such as the Cuban revolution of 1959, North Vietnam's victory in 1975, and the rise of the Sandinistas in 1979, complicate America's dealings with the USSR and increase the number and persuasiveness of the levers at the disposal of the Kremlin.

American strategy-making is complicated by a series of what might be called "cultural problems" with the Soviets:

- the delusion that we speak the same language;
- the delusion that we have the same vision of peace;
- the delusion that we can encourage the Soviets to change their behavior;
- the delusion that the Soviets are interested in a stable coexistence; and
- the delusion that there are moderates in the Kremlin whom we need to encourage and support.

This is a systemic problem in American foreign policy, and it is not a new one. Too many American policymakers, particularly those in the Foreign Service, are affected with what essayist Charles Krauthammer has labeled "solipsistic thinking," or the inability to conceive that foreigners could have different cultural viewpoints and biases. Arabists have been the classic example of this phenomenon. Too many of them have failed to acknowledge the profound differences in political culture that separate the United States from Arab and Islamic nations. Historically, Arabists have compounded the error by becoming apologists and interlocutors for the Arabs, explaining and advancing the Arab case on behalf of unconvertible and obdurate, yet somehow misunderstood clients.

Those who deal with the USSR, a nation remarkable for its cultural intractability and resistance to being "civilized" by Western standards, also are subject to solipsism and "clientitis." The failure to apprehend the profoundly alien and aggressively violent nature of Soviet and Russian political culture has prevented the United States from achieving the intellectual resolve to develop and commit to a long-term, far-reaching strategy against the USSR.

The Soviets appreciate how American ambivalence about the nature of the Soviet character can be used as a weapon against the United States. Since 1918, the Kremlin has periodically floated reports about closet moderates besieged by radicals within the Soviet leadership; of radical wings of the Communist party waxing in power because moderates were not given the ammunition by the West to justify a more accommodating policy; of new leaders, most recently Yuri Andropov and Gorbachev, who were closet "liberals" and admirers of Western literature and art; and of current leaders whose recent appreciation of Western liberalism, efficiency, or capitalist-style incentives needs only a few concessions to become a flame that would sweep away the detritus of the communist bureaucracy. What is astounding is not that after seventy years the Soviets still float such nonsense, but that after seventy years credulous American officials and experts swallow such lines *and adjust America's policies accordingly.*

This sort of behavior becomes rampant in times of superpower rapprochement, when the political fortunes of Western national leaders become inextricably linked with the "success" or "failure" of openings to the USSR. This phenomenon is also apparent when the Soviets are about to undergo or have just undergone a change in leadership. The Soviets are aware of this, of course, and they use such rumors to gain tactical and strategic advantages, including the paralysis of an American consensus and, for themselves, room and time to maneuver. This points up larger, functional problems that afflict the strategy-making processes of the United States, or the failure to

- achieve a consensus about the nature of the Soviet threat;
- conduct a threat assessment uncoupled from short-term political considerations;
- engage in long-perspective planning;
- establish policy continuity over administrations; and
- establish permanent political mechanisms, as well as military capabilities, to ensure against a continuation of these weaknesses.

Suffice it to say that on a systemic basis, the Soviets do not have any of these weaknesses. Furthermore, their system is innately aggressive and is structured to regularly carry out all of these functions associated with integrated political warfare.

Many of these institutional weaknesses might become more amenable to being remedied if a consensus about the nature of the Soviet threat were achieved in the United States. A signal failure of the Reagan administration has been the failure to better educate the American people and the Western allies about the nature of the Soviet threat. There certainly has been some progress on this score, but one cannot help but feel dissatisfied with how little the Reagan administration really has done. Too often, the Reagan administration has allowed the debate about U.S. policy toward the USSR to turn into a discussion of specific weapon systems or a parade of human interest stories. In a sense, the Reaganites shrank back from the responsibility of the mandate given them in 1980 to truly redefine the U.S.-Soviet relationship so that the United States would no longer find itself constantly undermined and exploited. One must conclude that the Reaganites—having conducted a decades-long dialectic about the specifics of the Soviet threat within the American political, foreign policy, and academic establishment—suddenly concluded upon coming to office that such "technicalitics," however persuasive to experts, could not be understood by ordinary Americans. Further, they apparently decided that a continuation of this already proven educational and dialectical approach would cause the eyes of politicians and media types to glaze over. In retrospect, this was a serious miscalculation.

Spectacular technological answers such as the B-1 and SDI may seem at first glance to be effective arguments. But lacking a context, they are not so persuasive. In fact, the American people can absorb and understand such seeming subtleties as Soviet disinformation, anti-Western Russian nationalism, Soviet support for international terrorism, Soviet violations of the ABM Treaty and the SALT II agreement, and the patterns and specifics of Soviet subversion. The classic Soviet response has been denial, obfuscation, countercharges, and disinformation. But instead of anticipating these actions and attempting to thwart them (and targeting the biggest uncritical conveyors of them in the media), the Reagan administration seems to have been buffaloed by the Soviet counterattack and by its own reliance upon shallow public relations.

Furthermore, the close association of the Reagan administration with military contractors benefiting from the Reagan buildup and its tolerance of waste and ineffective weapon systems has further vitiated the case for a more energetic strategy against the USSR. Finally, the Reagan administration's ill-conceived opening to Iran, the pattern of transparently compensatory statecraft that followed, and the culmination of the INF Treaty seriously undermined the administration's position as a principled exponent of a fundamental shift in U.S.-Soviet dealings.

The strongest ally of Americans seeking to change this nation's strategy-making remains the same: the Soviet Union itself. There are so many malefactions in which the Soviets engage, in so many areas both domestic and international, and on so many levels that one hardly need look for a trail of evidence to mount an incontrovertible case for a more effective strategy-making structure. But policymakers must not operate under the misimpression that the response to Soviet outrages will be self-evident or that the mechanism with which the West can mount its response will emerge spontaneously and with equal proof for the necessity of its very existence. Experience has already shown that things simply do not work out this way.

Given continuing Soviet aggression, therefore, would-be strategy-makers must aim at three mutually reinforcing objectives:

- the establishment of a permanent strategy-making mechanism;
- the facilitating of an ongoing consensus about the nature of the Soviet threat; and
- the instituting of an effective strategic response complete with the mechanisms that will enable it to survive over the change of administrations and the passage of decades.

CHAPTER 10

Toward a Strategy for Victory, I

To meet a continuing, increasingly aggressive Soviet threat, what kind of strategy should the United States and the West employ in the years ahead? The answer is undeniable: *We must aim at no less than a strategy for victory.* This is fundamental to the strategy-making process. Yet policymakers, attuned to short-term and politicized concerns, rarely confront the process directly, and public discussion is even more uncommon.

The nature of the threat posed by the Soviet Union makes any strategy that does not aim at victory unacceptable. The USSR, *glasnost* notwithstanding, shows no sign of abandoning its commitment to dialectical materialism and the class struggle. Such concepts are not merely words and fragments of empty ideology to the Soviet leadership: Practicalities may restrain their ability to achieve world domination, but their intent upon the ultimate goal has not waned.

The West must never forget what it confronts in the Kremlin: not theoretical and idealistic communists, but a carnivorous ruling group, bent on asserting their autocratic power on as wide a scale as possible. For them, this is a matter of legitimacy and identity, and each persona they assume—as communists, as inheritors of Lenin's will-to-rule, as managers of Stalin's state mechanism, and especially as Russians—only amplifies their aggressive and totalitarian aspirations. A strategy for victory, by its very enunciation, will put an end to the unproductive "reward and punishment" cycle of Western diplomacy toward the USSR. The Soviets heretofore have exploited the cyclical nature of this approach, making it the basis of both their periodic bursts of aggression and the diplomacy used to camouflage their actions.

As the only other superpower and as the only center of power capable of meeting the Soviet threat politically, economically, psycholog-

101

ically, and morally, the United States must possess a consistent counter-strategy. A consistent approach must be maintained even when there is an ongoing debate about the true intentions of one's adversary. Thus, a strategy for victory must put in place certain minimum yet effective elements guaranteed to remain in effect even while a larger strategic debate continues. This, in turn, requires a consensus that can transcend political shifts and changes in administration.

To some extent, such a consensus obviously exists; the United States has not abandoned its strategic forces nor its way of life in the face of Soviet blandishments. It has continued to maintain a defense capability designed to meet certain politico-military probabilities more or less adequately. Simultaneously, it has pursued strategic arms limitation diplomacy and its supposed benefits.

Yet given the concerted, carefully constructed and camouflaged nature of Soviet strategy, this sort of absurdist minimum is simply insufficient. Soviet gains do not truly materialize and solidify at the macro level. They are the cumulative product of many tactics tried and advantages seized on many fronts and in all the political dimensions of the Marxist-Leninist dialectic. Over time, an American consensus that is essentially reactive and defensive and that merely seeks to protect what the West already possesses against egregious Soviet assault must fail. With the initiative already conceded to the USSR, the Kremlin will inevitably consolidate its gains and maximize the return from the opportunities it seizes.

Is it possible for the Free World, the United States, and its allies to regain the initiative? Can the Free World mobilize its enormous strengths, which by any legitimate measure are superior to those of the Soviet slave empire? Can the Free World mobilize the collective will to throw this strength into the struggle and do so in time? The answer is yes. But making this answer into reality will be fraught with difficulty. Above all else, there must be an understanding, a basic recognition by the Free World that it is under purposeful attack—globally and by con-scious strategic design—and that the aggressor is determined to win by use of force if necessary, by the use of intimidation if possible.

A strategy for victory to meet this attack must meet five require-ments:

1) It must fully and correctly estimate the threat.
2) In the near term, it should be able to protect America's interests and positions.
3) In the long term, it must facilitate the projection of Western interests and the concomitant diminution of Soviet opportunities.
4) It should counter and neutralize Soviet tactics and strive to do so

with ever-increasing effectiveness.

5) It should systemically impede Soviet strategy and not open new avenues to Soviet adventurism. Moreover, it should undermine the assumptions and operational underpinnings on which Soviet strategy is based.

In contemplating an effective strategy for victory, one that can be implemented in the post-Reagan era, American policymakers will confront immediate challenges that must be met first. The most pressing of these challenges will derive from the legacy of the Reagan era: the Intermediate Nuclear Forces (INF) Treaty and the desultory development of the Strategic Defense Initiative.

THE INF TREATY

If an effective U.S. counterstrategy against Soviet aggression begins to work, we will see a heightened Soviet push for arms control diplomacy. Yet the proper prescription for this nation is becoming ever more apparent: the United States should separate itself from the arms control process. Furthermore, the process and the attendant political structure should be eliminated.

In view of the enlargement of the Soviet nuclear arsenal in recent years, nuclear arms control agreements based on the Soviet principle of "equality and equal security," in which the Soviet arsenal is equal to the sum of all other nuclear weapons in the world, endanger Western security in fundamental ways. The last twenty years demonstrate that the entire business of arms control diplomacy is a sham. It seems to be designed and structured by the USSR and Spenglerian Europeans to strip the West of its military and technical advantages over the Soviet system. The arms control process has proved itself to be fundamentally inimical to American security; therefore, we should reject strategic arms talks, negotiations, deals, and treaties as a matter of course.

The American president must educate the public to the deeper needs inherent in such a departure from conventional wisdom as this. He must proclaim that the problem is institutional, an endemic Soviet aggressiveness not only on the geopolitical stage but in the diplomatic arena as well; that the fundamental obstacle is Soviet aggression, combined with Soviet dishonesty and duplicity; and that the real problem is not the lack of better arms control agreements, nor the inability to achieve them, nor a lack of Soviet confidence in America. *On the contrary*, the USSR proceeds with arms control diplomacy because it has confidence that American politicians will sacrifice the long-term security of the

West for short-term political gains. It may be painful to recall the era, but the American people should be reminded of the fact that in the 1970s, at the height of the arms control process, Soviet aggression was also at its peak.

Given the aggressive and exploitive nature of the Soviet threat, America's leadership should internalize the fact that the Soviets will always outdo us, outmaneuver us, better us at arms control. Depending on what is appropriate, they will cheat, chisel, circumvent, take advantage of ambiguities, obfuscate, create ambiguities for future use, and discover new and unforeseen areas in which to gain an advantage. Conversely, when appropriate, they will strictly and ostentatiously observe the letter of the treaty in order to a) deflect criticism from other Soviet violations and b) deter legitimately beneficial American approaches to treaty interpretation.

The Intermediate Nuclear Forces Treaty, unlike the ABM Treaty, contains obvious strategic flaws, and its circumvention requires no obvious tactical ingenuity. The removal of the Pershing 2 and 1A from Western Europe will deprive NATO of its ability to launch a quick nuclear strike to deter a Soviet salient. The net effect will be the dismantling of the primary deterrent to Soviet aggression in Western Europe. Moreover, Western Europe will still be vulnerable to modern Soviet mobile missile systems, such as the SS-24 and SS-25. Finally, the enforcement of INF will leave NATO forces facing a five-to-one Warsaw Pact advantage in conventional forces. This will be a veritable invitation to invasion or, at minimum, to regular and growing Soviet intimidation of Western Europe. The likely long-term result of the INF Treaty will be the operative Finlandization of Western Europe. This cannot be regarded as "enhanced stability."

Confronted with the INF Treaty, the proper American response should not be an uncritical acceptance of the poisoned fruit of arms control diplomacy (its true nature revealed by the eager Soviet acceptance of the treaty). Rather, the United States should redouble its commitment to NATO and to the strategy that undergirds the very existence of the alliance.

Torn Western Alliance

Certainly, the negotiation of the INF Treaty and its provisions to strip Western Europe of its nuclear umbrella and open it to conventional Soviet power have dealt a body blow to the Western alliance. If left unreversed, the effect is likely to be manifested at the military, economic, and political levels. Now is the time for the United States to boost NATO and give conviction to the European hope that the United

States is still committed to European security. Now is *not* the time for the ratification and implementation of a profoundly ill-conceived and dangerous treaty.

The INF Treaty is so dangerous because it raises a fundamental question: How valid is the forty-year-old assumption that Western Europe needs alliances and military forces *in situ* in order to maintain its way of life and standard of living? By removing the American nuclear umbrella, the INF treaty raises the specter of U.S. isolationism; as a matter of necessity and survival, it is likely to trigger European isolationism and the development of a new diplomacy of Western Europe, keyed to the loss of the American nuclear shield, the possession of nuclear capabilities by Great Britain and France, and the desire for reunification by East and West Germany. The true issue raised by the INF Treaty, then, is not deterrence but *collective security*, which has profound military, political, economic, and strategic implications.

Let us posit certain intermediate-term outcomes from the implementation of the INF Treaty: What if the Europeans lose confidence in the United States or come to believe that we will negotiate above their heads on matters other than regional defense? Western Europe then might move toward an obeisant neutralism or toward a British-French-German security umbrella, or the Germans might move toward neutralism in the hope of reunification, leaving the defense of Western Europe to the British and French. The latter two outcomes would create a third, independent nuclear power. Immediately, it would constitute a new power center with which the USSR could negotiate independently. Over time, it would constitute a fully independent, economic and political center as well, eliminating the chance of a unified Western front against Soviet imperialism and calling into question the cultural and economic linkages that bind the West today.

The net effect of all this would be to force the United States from the continent and back to the Western Hemisphere, leaving the Europeans more vulnerable to Soviet pressure and less amenable to American suasion to a perceived or defined mutual interest. The Europeans certainly would feel greater pressure to accommodate to the USSR politically and allow themselves to supply and sustain the USSR economically or be parasitized economically.

While we assume that a European nuclear political force would be compliant toward the USSR, it is entirely possible that in time it could become aggressive and hostile toward the East and even the United States. This situation would resemble the circumstances that existed before 1914 when France and the United Kingdom were aligned against Germany. Based on this scenario, Western Europe in the future could be aligned against the USSR but less concertedly and persuasively than if done in coordination with a now-distrusted United States.

In light of the unilateral U.S. actions on INF, the United Kingdom and France, as nuclear powers, would attempt to deal *as nuclear powers* with the USSR on a theater basis. But this would be a weak approach, for the same abilities that enable the USSR to outmaneuver the United States tactically will be even more effective against the relatively limited geopolitical and economic options and strengths of the United Kingdom and France. (All this saying nothing for the potentials of intra-European rivalries, conflicts, and paralysis, stimulated or not by the USSR.)

West Germany's Retreat

Parts of Western and Eastern Europe might find themselves playing the role the Balkans played in the pre-World War I era. And it is possible that the Federal Republic of Germany, in the hope or name of reunification, might remove itself from this conflict. With the removal of the nuclear umbrella, the Germans might emerge as an Achilles' heel for a Western Europe that would find itself increasingly separated from the United States and increasingly menaced and parasitized by Soviet might. The German Right already believes that

1) reunification should be the first priority of the German nation;
2) the United States, as a polarizing power, of necessity is an impediment to this; and
3) the United States is not reliable and now is proving itself to be dangerous by conducting the INF negotiations and other contacts with the Soviets with insufficient consultation.

The German Left now claims that

1) it can deal with a genuinely more liberal, less threatening, *perestroika*-dedicated, *glasnost*-transformed USSR;
2) as Europeans dealing with Europeans [the Russians—*sic*.], it can do business with the Soviets in ways the United States cannot; and
3) the United States remains the primary threat to peace, and that this is more pronounced now with the rise of Gorbachev, whose liberalizing policies will always be vulnerable to attack by "doctrinaire Stalinists" because of reflexive American anticommunism.

The net effect of these attitudes would be a permanent sundering of the American-European alliance, which was achieved with so much bloodshed in two wars during this century. The rupture would be psychological, political, and economic as well as military. A divided Western Europe would face not only Balkanized and competitive politics, but a threat from the East unparalleled in modern times, a threat that would come to dominate all other considerations.

As a particularly odious variant, the Europeans might feel free to disparage U.S. power and deal with the USSR on the underlying assumption that U.S. military strength would come to the rescue, even as the Europeans would otherwise be encouraging its retreat and resigning themselves to its removal from the continent. But a United States constrained to act as merely a hemispheric power could not fulfill this sort of European wishful thinking. Moreover, as a hemispheric power, the United States would become increasingly habituated to *not* doing this. The same sort of psychological and economic rationales that justified American isolationism earlier in this century would reassert themselves. In time, the Soviets could not help but make a feast of the banquet of opportunities the INF Treaty would have created.

Could the United States accept a new center of power in Europe, a region for which we went to war twice in this century? Could we accept a separated and increasingly Balkanized Europe making its own strategic and economic deals with the USSR? On a larger scale, such an outcome would parallel the same type of strategic rollback the United States experienced in Vietnam with *twenty years of American policy investment destroyed*. In this instance, seventy years and an immense amount of blood and treasure spent in and on behalf of Europe stand to be discounted to the Soviets for no value by the political short-sightedness of the current administration.

Given this, INF represents a strategic retreat and a profound strategic change, with a unilateral abandonment of the very nuclear force that has held the Western defense, collective security, and a sense of collective unity and destiny together since World War II. And what would the ultimate impact of the INF treaty do to our long-standing insistence that the USSR must not dominate the land or the sea? The answers are truly terrifying to contemplate.

Can the United States then allow itself to become just a hemispheric power? Could it survive economically and politically as just a hemispheric power? We must note that even as the dominant force in the hemisphere, the United States is being challenged by the Soviets via Cuba and Nicaragua. In this context, Soviet strategy would acquire an increasing momentum, devouring and consolidating gains in both Europe and the Americas with ever-greater appetite and ferocity.

In pursuit of an extremely dubious, short-term gain represented by the INF Treaty, the Reagan administration is knocking out the under-

pinnings of collective Western security, the sense of collective enterprise, the belief in Western interdependence, and the hope of a shared
Western destiny, shared institutions, and shared values. *This is why the
Soviets have leaped on the INF Treaty.* It represents an easily achieved,
inexpensive opportunity to begin and simultaneously accelerate the dis-
lodging of U.S. military power and thus American political power and
influence from Western Europe. *If the INF Treaty is ratified and implemented, the United States will have neutralized itself.* A working
Western strategy must not permit this.

STRATEGIC DEFENSE INITIATIVE

There must be a major shift in U.S. and allied strategic planning and
power projection—which must include a survivable, second-strike nuclear
capability, enhanced conventional forces, and multilayered strategic
defense systems—or the Free World could be faced with politically prohibitive options of suicide or surrender. The Soviets are fast approaching the threshold of victory by intimidation to which the United States
could not effectively respond.

In this context, the Strategic Defense Initiative (SDI) must never be
a "bargaining chip." Significant elements of an effective strategic
defense system can and should be deployed forthwith. Yet reportedly
the centerpiece of a new U.S. position for the Geneva arms control
negotiations is an offer of seven-and-a-half years of only research and
development before any deployment. With strategic defense deployment
thus frozen, none of the scenarios presently on the bargaining table
contemplate an offensive weapons tradeoff so substantial as to reduce
meaningfully the Soviet first-strike capability. The Soviets have a
first-strike advantage now. They desire to acquire a strategic monopoly,
and this is why they continue to build their strategic forces. But
American strategic defense systems need not be leakproof in order to be
effective as a deterrent, either to a Soviet surprise strike or to Soviet
intimidation. Uncertainty about what the United States still would have
available in retaliation would itself, of course, constitute the deterrent.

It is clear that an effective strategy for victory must evolve under
the conditions of American repossession of a first-strike capability and
the implementation of the Strategic Defense Initiative. Simply put, if
SDI is conceded to the Soviets, then the United States will always be on
the defensive and will ultimately prove unsuccessful, no matter how
clever its other strategies may be. The United States has an obligation
to seek nothing less than unambiguous American military superiority.
This will require the development and full deployment of SDI.

With SDI, the United States will gain the following:

1) the reacquisition of a first-strike capability;
2) the capacity to deny the USSR the ability to wage large-scale conventional war on the basis of America's perceived willingness to use nuclear weapons;
3) the ability to block a nuclear attack from any quarter;
4) the capacity to block the credible threat of nuclear attack for political purposes; and
5) over time, the ability to nullify Soviet nuclear capability, *thus reducing conventional Soviet adventurism and aggression*.

None of the preceding capabilities will be achieved at once, or in total, but through the development and implementation of the SDI technologies and SDI's implicit strategies, they can be achieved progressively on an incremental basis. Moreover, with each passing year, particularly with the continued and growing implementation of SDI, the confidence of the Soviet Union will wane, just as American confidence gradually has waned heretofore in the face of continued Soviet gains.

If applied legitimately, something the Soviets would never agree to, arms control might lead to genuine force reductions. It might also prove useful in promoting Western strategy. But arms control can never be a substitute for a strategy. Soviet strategy demands that the USSR maintain the intimidation that its sole possession of a first-strike capability allows. While protecting this, the USSR seeks to deny the United States influence over Soviet decision-making, and implementation of the Strategic Defense Initiative would give the United States such influence. Moreover, if the USSR continues to be the sole superpower with a first-strike capability, then it is more likely to be more aggressive on the regional/geopolitical level. Thus, SDI, like investments in conventional forces in a nuclear age, should be seen as a commitment that will pay a dividend in the real world and whose impact will not be merely theoretical.

As noted earlier, SDI also would strip the USSR of its conventional force strength (via the deployment of terrestrial kinetic weapons using SDI technologies) and would further strain it economically, by forcing a tremendous new investment in the next generation of tanks, artillery, short-range missiles, and so on. All this would mean a sharp, intermediate-term diminution of the Soviet threat and of the Soviet intimidation quotient.

But all that SDI promises is now at risk. The desultory American approach to the full development of SDI and its associated technologies renders the American ability to act as an effective counterweight against

Soviet power open to question. The USSR currently possesses a first-strike capability against much of our Triad—our ICBM land force, half our SLBM force, and 70 percent to 80 percent of our bombers on the ground. Within half an hour to launch, the Soviets can eliminate the American retaliatory capability and hold the reserves to intimidate the United States into nonretaliation. *This condition compromises all of our security commitments throughout the world and in every theater. Conversely, it emboldens the Soviet Union toward greater adventurism on a geopolitical scale.* It undermines the sense of security commitment between the United States and its allies and undermines the credibility of our international commitments as a whole.

The ratification and implementation of the INF Treaty will only amplify this reality. Furthermore, the implementation of a Strategic Arms Reduction Talks (START) Treaty as now envisioned, eliminating half of the fixed American missiles while permitting the Soviets to double their projected missile-kill ratio with mobile SS-24 and SS-25 ICBMs, would further undermine America's security and credibility. Taken together, INF, START, and the failure to deploy SDI would catastrophically erode America's ability to guarantee the security of the Western alliance and, concomitantly, to restrain Soviet aggression in the conventional sphere.

Over time, the failure to deploy SDI fully will do away with extended deterrence. It will increasingly threaten the mutual confidence upon which practical collective security is based. In time, failure to deploy SDI and thus neutralize the Soviet first-strike capability will enable the Soviet Union to break out from the restraints imposed upon it by Western action up until now. Increasingly contemptuous of America's strategic deterrent and increasingly unconcerned about concerted Western retaliation, the USSR will move to circumvent the choke points in the Far East, the Middle East, and the North. It will accelerate its drive to acquire warm-water ports in the Persian Gulf and the Indian Ocean. This would enable the USSR to threaten oil supplies to Western Europe, further amplifying Soviet strategic influence.

Moreover, the American failure to maintain a credible deterrent will encourage the USSR to increase its economic contacts with regard to the resources and facilities in Soviet East Asia and free itself from NATO choke points and from the threat of unacceptable damage on the Soviet homeland that might otherwise be inflicted by the West. In doing this, the USSR will find the one means by which it can compensate for its current internal economic weakness *without* having to liberalize economic policies or centralized party control. Each Soviet success here will set the stage for further Western weakening and new Soviet salients. The ultimate result of this will materialize as discussed earlier:

The Soviet Union will be able to move in places as it chooses, at the time of its choosing, with increasing confidence, and eventually with impunity.

Thus, the foremost objective of American strategy must be to deny the USSR a free hand to *forge new correlations of power* throughout the world. This requires the full deployment of SDI *and* a restoration of our retaliatory capability at the nuclear level in a manner that *personally* threatens the Soviet political and military leadership and the means of coercion and legitimacy upon which the Communist party relies for its survival. Only this will prove persuasive to the Soviets and truly restrain Soviet adventurism and exploitative behavior, enabling an American counterstrategy to operate effectively.

SYSTEMIC APPROACHES TO VICTORY

A strategy for victory can only be mounted by a system geared for victory. There are a number of systemic changes that a strategy for victory should implement.

Aggregate Threat Assessment

As noted earlier, the Soviet Union does not pursue its adventurism on a single front. On the contrary, the USSR frequently moves in similar ways to exploit particular systemic weaknesses on a number of fronts. Moreover, the Soviet Union evaluates its position on an aggregate basis. It views the world as a seamless, single arena in which the fundamental class struggle is played out.

In contrast, American threat assessment and the tactics resulting from that assessment are highly compartmentalized. The Department of State and the Central Intelligence Agency assign most work to offices devoted to specific regions or nations. Executives at the top may make an effort to achieve a wider view, but the factors that shape actual decision-making—the papers that presage conclusions, the interactions of personnel that animate discussions, even the mundane aspects of internal administration—are all affected by their point of origin within the institutional structure. This is a fact of bureaucratic life.

The net effect of compartmentalization is twofold. On the one hand, those within the structure find themselves in a competition with their counterparts for the attention of the top administrators and the allocation of resources to their offices and their region. Parochialism increases and cooperation plummets, removing the incentive for assuming a broader viewpoint. On the other hand, senior administrators (who cannot ignore any institutional division entirely) feel obligated to placate and accommodate each office to some extent. Over time, this reinforces the institutional culture and validates the belief that narrowness gets results. As bureaucrats who have acquitted themselves well in these intramural struggles rise to executive positions, this attitude becomes entrenched. The ability and inclination of administrators to seek a synthesis is further diminished; parochialism drives out catholicity.

American policymakers could better anticipate which areas will be of interest to the Soviet Union if they could better consider Soviet internal needs and derived priorities. The dimensions of the Soviet threat are such that the United States can no longer afford not to have a high-level office devoted to aggregate threat assessment. Such a body would collect and integrate a wide range of raw intelligence, regional analyses, economic assessments, and other information to produce an integrated picture of Soviet activities worldwide. This office would identify trends in Soviet techniques and initiatives, flagging potential problems that the Soviets might be moving to exploit on a multiregional basis. An aggregate threat assessment office also would track and compare episodes of Soviet adventurism. Aware of the pattern of past Soviet moves in similar situations, policymakers could test possible responses and then could initiate countermoves with a higher degree of confidence.

An aggregate threat assessment office would regularly synthesize an estimate of Soviet aggression worldwide. This would illuminate the priorities attached to each region *by the Soviets* and enable American policymakers to make better judgments of where to make political investments and where to exercise restraint. An aggregate threat assessment would also enable an administration to tailor responses by quality and complexity as well as size to a particular region. Knee-jerk and ill-considered stock responses, such as the simple military demonstrations that have characterized much of recent American power projection, could be avoided unless appropriate.

In addition, an aggregate threat assessment office could give policymakers a true understanding of the overall balance in the world and enable them to judge what events had truly damaged or enhanced America's position and what responses and counterresponses had had a similar effect. Finally, the mere existence of an aggregate threat assessment office would sober the Soviets about American intentions and capabilities and have a restraining effect. Moreover, the favor and confidence accrued by the office would encourage the foreign policy and intelligence establishments to exercise a broader and more synthetic world view. It would establish within the institutional culture a selective advantage for intramural *cooperation*. Over time, this would have a distinctly positive effect upon America's strategy-making capabilities.

Consensus Maintenance

As noted repeatedly, American strategy toward the USSR, such as it is, moves in fits and starts. Each change in presidential administrations brings with it new emphases and priorities in the relationship with the USSR. Nearly every congressional election spells a change of mood, as reflected in the perceived national attitude about the Soviets. Changes in the Soviet leadership have had an even greater effect both in the United States and in Western Europe. Each recent shift has occasioned a flood of hopeful articles in the Western press and optimistic speeches by public officials and by (often ill-informed) molders of public opinion.

The Kremlin has become a master of manipulating Western opinion on this score. In 1982, the KGB had many Americans believing Yuri Andropov—a former KGB chief—was a closet liberal. Gorbachev's public relations salient at the December 1987 Washington summit was a masterpiece of agitprop and manipulation within an enemy bourgeois democracy. The net effect of this process is a weakening of American resolve in the on-again, off-again pursuit of remedies to Soviet adventurism.

If the United States can synthesize the totality of the Soviet threat worldwide, then the next logical step should be the articulation of a minimum set of countermoves to meet that threat. This minimum should not be dependent upon any superficial and suspect change in Soviet behavior. Rather, the integrated Western response to the Soviet threat should only be adjusted when the totality of Soviet aggression has been observed to have materially and permanently diminished. Until that time, the West should continue to implement this minimum set of responses and do so in an unwavering fashion. Indeed, the Western response should be maintained at considerably more than the minimum level.

Given the existence of an aggregate threat assessment office, a U.S. administration would find it less difficult to make its case for a consistent global strategy against the Soviet Union. Both Congress and the NATO allies would find it easier to agree about policy; concomitantly, they would find it more difficult to argue for what would be seen as an unjustified softening toward the Kremlin. Policymakers have an obligation to build an ongoing consensus at home and abroad about the dimensions of the Soviet threat and the means by which the United States and the West are moving to meet it.

If a consensus is achieved and maintained, a steadier response will be effected year to year and decade to decade. In addition, policy disagreements will focus not on the fundamentals of the Western response, as is now the case, or on whether an energetic response is really justified at all. Rather, such debates will focus on two things: first, whether the minimal level of an already effective U.S. response to Soviet adventurism, the so-called "ground state," ought to be raised; and second, what means the United States should utilize to increase the effectiveness of its response to the Soviet world threat.

The United States should aim at achieving a consensus that is logical and ineluctable. In addition to utilizing an aggregate threat assessment office, there are other things policymakers in the United States can do to build consensus. For example, a permanent Team B can be established for making estimates about the USSR. The ramifications of this are discussed below.

Second, policymakers can arrive at an integrated picture of the global Soviet threat and disseminate it both domestically and abroad. It is remarkable how few otherwise-informed people perceive the actual dimensions and coordinated aspects of Soviet aggression. An aggregate threat assessment, properly presented, can only build the consensus for action to meet the Soviet threat. It should not be assumed that the global dimensions of the Soviet design are apparent or even obvious to Western opinion.

Also, specific policies should be linked and identified as being part of a minimum set of answers to Soviet aggression. So characterized, these policies will gain a stature and permanence by virtue of their group identity and the reinforcement they supposedly provide for each other. This will not be a simple undertaking, but American policymakers bent on achieving a strategic consensus must not assume that the justification for specific initiatives is any more self-evident than the global Soviet threat these initiatives are designed to halt.

Policymakers should also try to focus the strategic debate on increments *above* the minimum set of responses and not on the policies that comprise that minimum. This is a matter of spin control and practical politics. But if over time an administration's policymakers characterize certain policies as not subject to debate and inextricably linked to other responses to the USSR, then the political struggle will inevitably shift to issues that appear to be still open to debate. The Reagan administration was able to do this with the emplacement of cruise missiles and Pershings in Western Europe, the 600-ship navy, the construction of large nuclear carriers, the desirability of the Midgetman, and SDI research. Being able to operate this way is a simple and essential test of leadership.

Finally, led by the president and mindful of the global dimensions of the Soviet threat, leaders of both the Democratic and Republican parties should formally engage in meetings to define a national consensus on a counterstrategy to the USSR. It is generally assumed that the decision of the electorate and the actions of the president establish this consensus. But this is precisely what is responsible for the erratic nature of the American position, something that unnecessarily assists the USSR with every passing decade.

There is considerable respect within Congress for the larger responsibilities of the nation. There is also a desire, born of an aversion to assuming blame for potential setbacks, for the diffusion of responsibility about national security. At pains to depoliticize the issue, the president could use these psychological and political realities to promote an ongoing conference to achieve and articulate a consensus. The minimum aspects of the American counterstrategy could certainly be agreed upon and identified. Though the result might be limited, even this small achievement would then promote further consensus among the Western allies. It would also nurture the consensus-building process domestically and within the Western alliance.

The Establishment of a Permanent "Team B"

The "Team B" of the 1970s was a radical departure for American strategy-making. It was an institutionalized riposte to conventional wisdom, an institutionalized mechanism of achieving an alternate threat assessment. Team B took nothing about the USSR as a given, except the certainty of opposition from within the foreign policy establishment to any iconoclastic opinions it might voice. Nonetheless, Team B concluded that the USSR had launched a massive buildup of strategic weapons, in a clear violation of the assumptions of détente. This had a profound effect upon America's attitudes, though the effect did not fully manifest itself until half a decade after Team B completed its work.

Team B's legacy is incomplete, because the concept of a Team B did not survive the initial experiment. The Team B concept put great strain on a bureaucratic system committed to unified national estimates and hostile to minority opinions because of their potential political ramifications. Yet the United States continues to impair its own security by its refusal to establish the Team B concept not only for macro geopolitical estimates but for regional estimates as well.

In current practice, managers of foreign policy and intelligence analysis put together estimate teams that produce assessments and recommendations that are endorsed by desk officers or heads of branches. These managers generally try to assemble teams in which there will be a diversity of opinion and a productive mix of different skills. Minority opinions are tolerated, particularly in the early stages of an assessment, but there is an institutional predilection for consensus in both analysis and recommendations. The inability to achieve a consensus is perceived as a confession of management weakness and as a failure to complete the assignment. It also serves as an invitation to institutional one-upmanship from competing divisions within the bureaucracy.

The greater good at issue here is the security of the nation, not survival within the bureaucracy. To meet this problem, the United States has an obligation to change the way in which national intelligence estimates are made. The institutional value attached to consensus and certainty should be downgraded. Estimates should be divided into issue areas in which there is high confidence, moderate confidence (for the reasons noted) and low confidence (with the factors fully identified). Similarly, the facets of each analyses should be qualified as to whether they represent unanimous opinion or majority opinion (with the position of the minority laid out in equal detail, along with its reasons).

This will require a revision of mores in the bureaucratic culture, which is easier said than done. Yet if policymakers demonstrate that they wish to consider all alternatives and that a full discussion of the possibilities will be bureaucratically rewarded—in preference to a putative consensus advanced with false confidence—then the intelligence and foreign policy communities will begin generating analyses and estimates that have the Team B mentality already incorporated. Policymakers relying upon such estimates will be able to choose from a more diverse, finely graded set of responses to Soviet actions. They will also have a sense of those areas in which they can move with confidence and those areas in which they should exercise particular circumspection.

Permanent Teams B should be established in key areas of foreign policy, military estimate, and intelligence analysis. Staffers who first serve on a primary estimate and analysis team and then on a Team B will gain a greater appreciation of the need to question conventional wisdom and to test seemingly safe assumptions. They will also gain an institutional empathy for those who question the majority position, thus encouraging the development of an institutional culture that is more tolerant of iconoclasts. It should also serve as an incentive to the foreign policy and intelligence agencies to become true marketplaces of ideas, where the value of divergent opinions can be honestly determined. America's strategy-making and its ability to anticipate and respond to diverse Soviet threats can only stand to gain.

On the macro scale, a Team B for evaluating the Soviet threat should be reestablished as a permanent part of the American policymaking establishment. American leaders will be able to make more-informed, less-politicized choices in policy initiatives. In those situations that are subject to intense debate, policymakers will have the option of legitimizing an inferential median between the extremes of opinion.

The existence of a permanent Team B for Soviet threat estimates will mean that a broader spectrum of opinion is incorporated into American policymaking. The entire strategic debate thus will be less subject to politicization, no matter whether the administration in office is liberal or conservative. In turn, this is likely to increase the steadiness of American policy and diminish the chance of sudden and disruptive shifts in attitude toward the USSR; therefore, the overall effectiveness of the American counterstrategy will also increase. Most important of all, this new stability will make it easier to articulate and maintain a consensus about the true dimensions of the Soviet threat and a consensus about the minimum means by which the United States should meet that threat.

A Permanent National Strategy Office

As discussed in the preceding chapter, the United States has profound shortcomings in its strategy-making processes for it lacks a unified national strategy office as well as a unified national strategy. Over the long term, a superpower bearing the responsibilities as those of the United States cannot function effectively in a competition with the Soviet Union without a permanent mechanism with which to achieve and hone a national strategy. Part of the executive branch should be specifically charged with integrating the immense amount of intelligence and political analysis the United States generates into an integrated national strategy.

Such an office should be something like a center for advanced study, bringing together diverse talents and iconoclastic minds and allowing them to interact freely. The participation of outside experts—political scientists, economists, historians, psychologists—should be encouraged as an institutional value. In this way, a reserve of expertise can be initiated and nurtured, endowing the nation with a skilled and self-sustaining cadre of individuals trained in strategy-making. The relevant models here should be the Manhattan Project, the early Atomic Energy Commission, the War Colleges or the Office of Strategic Services (OSS), and other elite organizations that gathered and engaged the best minds from a wide range of backgrounds in free inquiry and created entire schools and disciplines. Members of Congress and the military also should be involved fully in the work of the strategy office. Assuring their ongoing participation will lay the groundwork for greater consensus-building on a variety of issues relating to national security. The beneficial effects of this will increasingly manifest themselves over time, as more individuals come to feel that they have an institutional, personal, and political stake in the maintenance of a steady national strategy.

The focus of a national strategy office should be on "Grand Strategy," operating strategies, and microstrategies for specific regions. Tactics would be gamed and evaluated in light of Soviet actions and perceived Soviet intentions. Obviously, a national strategy office would work closely with an aggregate threat assessment office, just as the CIA, the NSA, and the National Reconnaissance Office cooperate in channeling information and suggesting areas of attention. A national strategy office would give the managers of foreign policy the precise means with which to actually implement the often-neglected essentials of strategic foreign policy (discussed at the end of chapter eleven under the subheading, *A Strategy for Engagement*).

The national strategy office would have three overriding objectives:

1) to derive, validate, test, and constantly improve an overall national strategy complete with implementing tactics (to ensure maximum effectiveness in this task and to promote national consensus about the overall strategy, the national strategy office would have its own Team B);
2) to integrate the strengths and strategies of various U.S. agencies, including the armed services, the State Department, the intelligence agencies, and the Treasury and Commerce departments into that national strategy; and
3) to encourage these agencies to think strategically and cooperate with them in developing operating and microstrategies that would complement and implement the overall national strategy.

Even if the national strategy office acts initially only as a clearinghouse, resource base, and training facility for other branches of government, it will do much to stabilize America's responses to Soviet aggression and improve this nation's ability to operate effectively in the world. Its very existence will demonstrate a willingness to challenge and reverse Soviet gains and the intent to convince the USSR that American efforts in this regard are serious and not temporary. In full operation, the national strategy office will give the United States a powerful means to promote the cause of freedom.

CHAPTER 11

Toward a Strategy
for Victory, II

In confronting the Soviet threat, the United States should follow a combination of mutually reinforcing traditional and innovative approaches. Each should be designed to accomplish the following goals:

1) attack the Soviet Union *systemically*,
2) stress the Soviet Union economically, socially, psychologically, ideologically, and militarily,
3) target Soviet vulnerabilities,
4) elicit caution from the Soviet leadership,
5) undermine as much as possible the legitimacy of the *nomenklatura*,
6) force the Soviet leadership to evaluate options in terms of how they might affect continued control by the CPSU,
7) undermine the enforced unity of the Soviet state,
8) neutralize past Soviet gains, while making Soviet initiatives to recapture them as economically difficult as possible,
9) impose high-risk scenarios upon Soviet decision-making,
10) deny the easy availability of low-risk alternatives,
11) strain the ties between the USSR and its vassals and clients,
12) lower the confidence that Soviet allies have in the Kremlin,
13) increase the attractiveness of the Western democratic model,
14) promote economic and psychological separation from Moscow, and
15) suggest an image of continuing, ineluctable Western success at the expense of those who hew closely to the Kremlin.

Future U.S. strategies should include elements outlined here in order for America to meet its responsibilities as a superpower in guaranteeing freedom in the Western world.

STRATEGIC AND CONVENTIONAL MILITARY BUILDUP

No strategy can substitute for the empirical means with which to implement that strategy, to project power, and to defend interests. The military buildup during the Reagan years has restored some of the capabilities that were allowed to dwindle during previous administrations, yet the United States still commits less than 6.5 percent of its gross national product to defense, compared with a probable 20 percent to 25 percent directly and indirectly for the USSR. Over time, even an inefficient economy such as that of the USSR can achieve an overwhelming advantage in numbers and depth of systems. The United States will confront this threat through the end of the century.

A discussion about a strategic and conventional buildup should do more than focus narrowly on the merits of specific weapon systems. Instead, we should consider the strategic objectives such a buildup should aim at achieving.

The Reacquisition of a First-Strike Capacity in Terms That Are Politically Persuasive to the Soviet Leadership

As noted earlier, the American first-strike capacity must deter Soviet aggression. If the Soviets believe that the Leninist system can survive a nuclear exchange, then the intent behind our strategic war capacity will have failed. The Soviets target American ICBMs because they seek to deny the United States the ability to affect the decision-making process of the CPSU leadership. This being the case, the American first-strike capacity should target the Soviet leadership in such a way as to make their concerns about their *survival in power* too problematical to risk the initiation of hostilities.

In *Survival Is Not Enough*, Pipes suggests that American forces target the command centers and shelters of the *nomenklatura*. He observes that the ability to threaten the survival and control of the Soviet leadership should be the *primary* criterion by which American strategic sufficiency is determined. America's strategic missile forces should not target the civilian population, he writes, but

> the true culprits of such aggression, the *nomenklatura* and its armed forces. Specialists estimate that there are in the Soviet Union 10,000 to 20,000 objectives of political and military significance. If that assessment is correct, then the United States needs that many accurate warheads left *after absorbing a first strike*; this capability alone will provide a deterrent credible to Moscow [Emphasis in original].

One could observe that if the United States possessed such a capability, the Soviet propaganda claim that all would die in a nuclear exchange would truly be accepted by the Soviet leadership.

The Acquisition of Nuclear, Chemical, and Biological Weapon Systems Capable of Meeting a Wide Range of War Conditions and of Accomplishing a Range of Military Objectives

The United States has allowed itself to accept the Soviet argument that the use of nuclear weapons must inevitably escalate into a full-scale, mutually suicidal nuclear exchange. Yet the Soviets continue to pursue weapon systems that give them a fineness of effect and a versatility the United States lacks. Ratifying the INF Treaty will further exacerbate this American weakness.

Nuclear devices are conceived to enhance the persuasiveness of a nation's political position. In a sense, they invert the Clausewitzian doctrine about war and politics: Nuclear weapons are war by other means. The increasing reliance upon massive strategic forces as the sole nuclear weapon in the American arsenal means that the United States cannot bring the nuclear argument to bear on the regional or micro level. Conversely, the Soviets continue to utilize and develop nuclear weapons in a wide range of formats in order to provide themselves with the political ability to use their nuclear capability to reinforce their political activities at the local level. Their development of chemical and biological weapons enhances this capacity; so does their perceived willingness to use a variety of political tactics eschewed by the United States.

American policymakers should recognize that so-called tactical-nuclear and theater-nuclear devices exist not only to give generals the ability to make bigger noises. They are serious devices for implementing strategy, for they establish a superpower *as a superpower* at a variety of levels of engagement and increase the intimidation/persuasion factor that often enables strategies to succeed simply by their clear articulation.

The United States needs to develop weapons systems capable of meeting a wide range of war conditions and military objectives. Thus America should step up development, production, and deployment of a wider range of nuclear devices, especially Enhanced Radiation Devices (so-called neutron bombs). The administration should be prepared to make the strategic argument for such weapons and should develop the intellectual case that forcefully rejects the Soviet contention that escalation is inevitable.

For similar reasons, the accelerated development of chemical and biological weapons should be pursued. Concomitant with this, the United States should make the development of defense mechanisms against these devices a top priority. Chemical and biological systems are already part of the Soviet arsenal. They have been tested and honed in Cambodia, Afghanistan, and Ethiopia. Like infantrymen charging the first machine gun nests, the United States should not assume that either élan or will alone can triumph over the tactical reality established by our enemy. Only anticipation, preparation, and the concerted application of winning force can accomplish this.

The Rapid Development and Full Deployment of the Strategic Defense Initiative

These factors are necessary for the reasons discussed above.

A Numerical Expansion of American Sea Power, Beginning with Carrier Task Forces

Events of the last two decades have demonstrated that nothing is as effective in projecting American influence and protecting American interests as a nuclear-powered carrier (CVN) task force. Comprising the one nuclear-capable, strategic weapon system that is called fully into action on a regular basis, such carrier groups are fully self-sustaining, self-protecting mobile bases. They can execute all the facets of a military operation, including

- establishing and maintaining a political presence;
- supporting allies ashore;
- intelligence collection;
- early warning and reconnaissance;
- command, communications, and control;
- logistical support, loading and unloading;
- perimeter and area defense;
- amphibious attack;
- offshore shelling and skirmishing;
- long-range and short-range aerial attack; and
- classical naval warfare.

The United States now possesses more carrier task forces than it could deploy at the beginning of the Reagan era, but most of the carriers, including the nuclear-powered U.S.S. *Enterprise*, are in the middle of their useful lives or are approaching the end. Carrier task forces are also hampered by a less than adequate number of support ships and an insufficient complement of personnel. Because nothing is as important year to year in the actual projection of American influence as the carrier-based task force, because additional missions that CVNs can and should be fulfilling exist right now, because the need for CVN-based projection of geopolitical strategy will increase in the next two decades, and because the USSR is moving to a nuclear, carrier-based force projection capability, the next U.S. president should embark upon a program that features the following:

1) U.S. naval forces should be expanded to eighteen carrier task forces, fully equipped and fully manned.
2) All carriers that will be thirty years old through 1998-2002 should be rapidly replaced. All replacements should be nuclear powered, and the still-battleworthy ships they replace should be deployed in smaller tactical task forces and/or held as reserves to replace CVNs during dry-docking and refitting. Because of their immense strategic usefulness, even when they no longer can completely fulfill the roles assigned today to CVNs, older carriers as a matter of course should not be decommissioned.
3) The U.S. Navy must concentrate on increased readiness and fitting out of each carrier task force, so that the United States can get maximum use of its investment for the purposes of power projection and protection of our interests and allies.

Improvement of the "Teeth-to-Tail" Ratio of NATO Forces

This factor is concomitant with the complete standardization of all equipment in the NATO inventory.

Complete Standardization of Equipment and Systems Among the U.S. Armed Services and Among the NATO Allies Would Be Indispensable, Given the Overwhelming Superiority in Conventional Forces Enjoyed by the Warsaw Pact

The INF Treaty, if approved, would make these improvements mandatory. If the United States and its NATO allies are to confront the Warsaw Pact in conventional terms, then a sort of super-Israeli model must be followed and soon.

Western conventional forces may yet have real deterrent effect upon the Warsaw Pact if they are perceived to be far superior and more battle capable than their communist counterparts. Given the crucial geopolitical role they must play, the armed forces defending Western

Europe must be trained and equipped as if they were elite fighting units. Indeed, the United States and its allies should apply the standards for elite units to every military unit in Western Europe. Support staff should be kept to a minimum, while readiness and mobility should be at a peak. Required skill levels for all personnel should be much more demanding than in the past. Ongoing political education should inculcate a clear sense of mission and initiative, self-reliance, and innovation should be studied and practiced. Functional integration between large and small units of both U.S. and NATO forces should be as complete as possible. Finally, officers should become more battle practiced and tested in advance to become oriented to direct involvement in front-line battle leadership instead of rear-echelon "battle management" (an oxymoron, at best).

Applied over time to units in Western Europe, such improvements should become the model for all American and, ideally, Western military forces. Faced with smaller conventional force capabilities and given the critical role assigned to units in Western Europe, NATO nations should apply the same kind of standards for conventional warfare used by Israel, a militarily outnumbered nation whose very survival depends upon competent military performance. Such improvements will benefit Western strategy and force projection by deterring Soviet aggression in Western Europe and around the globe. American military units, once they have achieved elite levels of fighting and operational prowess, can be expected to perform in theater operations with a competence not demonstrated in similar circumstances during the 1970s and 1980s. Over time, exemplary performances and the avoidance of such debacles as Desert One and the Beirut Marine barracks massacre should discourage adventurism by both the USSR and its clients.

THE APPLICATION OF AMERICAN STRENGTHS AGAINST SOVIET WEAKNESSES

The ancient Chinese military analyst Chang Yü observed, "Take advantage of the enemy's unpreparedness; attack him when he does not expect it; avoid his strength and strike his emptiness. . . ."

Western strategy makers should assess, carefully and fully, where the USSR is vulnerable and where the United States has particular strengths. The United States should then shape its policies in order to exacerbate these Soviet weaknesses. If adhered to assiduously and managed with imagination and skill, such an approach will quickly elicit caution and circumspection from the Kremlin. Over time, it may permanently alter the equation of the U.S.-Soviet confrontation in favor of the West. At minimum, it will reverse the current situation in which the USSR operates as if any aspect of the West is a target of opportunity while simultaneously giving the message that a commensurate salient against the USSR will quickly lead to nuclear holocaust.   Utilizing Western strengths against Soviet weaknesses is the quickest and most effective way of discrediting the psychological terrorism that is at the core of Soviet policy.   More important, operating this way will advance and define a "Grand Strategy of the West," deriving directly from the characteristics of democratic capitalism.

An Economic Strategy

In the face of an emerging Soviet market, the president must determine that it is not in the American interest to subsidize the survival of a weak yet oppressive Soviet leadership.   Otherwise, this will mimic the West's self-destructive dealings with OPEC but on a larger, more permanent, more dangerous scale.

The net effect of the rationalizations and pusillanimity that characterized relations with OPEC in the 1970s was a dislocation of much of the world's economy.   When we look at OPEC today, however, it emerges now that its members were both avaricious and uncreative.   The OPEC states squandered nearly all of the political capital they accumulated during the oil boom and much of their financial capital as well. The Soviets will not be so stupid, so short-sighted or so transient. They know how to use capital for industrial development and not for self-indulgence.   Moreover, there was a limit on how much the West could become dependent on OPEC; high oil prices brought more oil into the market and lessened our dependence.   The Western democracies' status as the Soviet Union's economic tributary will not fade away so easily, if at all.

The Arabs of OPEC could only threaten consumers in an Adam Smithian fashion: they would raise the price or limit supplies.   But the Soviets have a military threat, and the longer a parasitical economic relationship is maintained, the more credible that military threat will become, *because the Soviet military increasingly adapts and utilizes Western industrial gains brought to the USSR to speed its military development even further*.   Moreover, unlike the Arabs' economic threats, the USSR's military threat is only barely challengeable (and the Soviets move every way they can to make it even less so).   Thus, it is important for American strategy to minimize Western financing of the Soviet economy and to monitor technology transfer carefully.   The net effect of these actions will be to delay (and ideally, increasingly slow) the Soviet military buildup, which is based qualitatively on the acquisition of Western technology and the infusion of Western capital. In turn, this will make it more difficult for the Soviets to establish and sustain their economic base in the East, something that otherwise will validate their military strategy. Denying the Soviets easy trade and credit will challenge and circumscribe their strategy on a permanent basis.

Soviet strategy strives to compensate for Soviet weaknesses by intimidating and parasitizing the West. Clearly, the greatest Soviet weakness is economic. To defeat Soviet strategy, the United States must exacerbate the weaknesses of the Soviet economy. By doing so relentlessly, the United States will not elicit a Soviet military attack, as the Soviets have threatened and as some pusillanimous appeasers have feared. Rather, the United States will create a circumspect USSR, one much less given to adventurism and much more cautious in its external conduct.

Given the scope of Soviet activities, one must question how the Soviet economy, inefficient as it is, finances Soviet aggression on a worldwide scale. The answer is Soviet adventurism is not self-financing. The USSR is now at a breakout point in its use of *Western money* to support its Marxist-Leninist designs. Unless the Western governments act soon, the Soviet Union, acting directly and through agents, will be able to insinuate itself permanently into the financial structure of the West. It then will be able to extract ever-greater amounts of capital to support and expand its imperialism, making the West pay for its own demise, as it were.

PlanEcon Research Associates, a Washington-based think tank, forecasts that Soviet external debt will increase 80 percent by the early 1990s. By that time, the USSR may have more than $100 billion in loans outstanding to the West, a figure already accrued for the Soviet bloc as a whole. Such a level of indebtedness would normally affect a nation's credit rating and would entitle banks to greater amounts of information from the borrowing country. It would also entitle the creditors to a greater say in the economic policy of the country. But institutionalized Soviet obfuscation of its credit and banking status is designed to minimize Western say over Soviet economic policy while maximizing the USSR's ability as a putatively low-debt nation to maneuver within the international financial system and exploit it further. Coming and going, the power of the communist leadership to act unilaterally and unchecked will be protected and, indeed, increased.

Loans to the Soviet Union today come in two forms. First of all, monies guaranteed by Western governments account for about 45 percent of loan amounts to the USSR. Such loans are used to finance goods, services, and projects exported from or provided by a Western nation to the Soviet Union and/or the Eastern Bloc. Then the Soviets have taken advantage of so-called "untied loans," which are open lines or transfers of credit. They are made for no specific purpose, have few conditions attached to how the monies are to be used, and are often repaid over extended periods of time and at low rates. These deals total about 55 percent of the loan amounts to the Soviet Union. They include loans for construction and industrial projects where the life of the loan exceeds the life or start-up period of the project and loans made for projects that never seem to get built.

Despite the fact that Western banks have curtailed sharply untied lending to country borrowers worldwide since the 1970s, the USSR continues to enjoy access to undisciplined Western credits, especially those from European and Japanese banks, with little or no serious attempt on the part of Western banks to either verify or monitor the actual use of their funds. These loans can be and are used by the Soviets for any purpose, including the support of client states, the underwriting of terrorism, and the facilitation of weapons transfers to enemies of the West. These loans are also used in the Soviet recycling scheme: A series of transfers between Western banks and financial institutions directly or indirectly controlled by the Soviet Union are used to make Western capital appear as Soviet assets. This sleight of hand is structured to exploit bank reporting procedures. It is worth billions of dollars to the USSR annually, decreasing apparent Soviet indebtedness and creating phantom Soviet financial strength, all the while increasing the apparent indebtedness of the West to the Soviet bloc.

Even more threatening now is the fact that in the near future the Soviets hope to issue Euronotes and bonds for the first time, thereby recruiting additional Western financial institutions, such as pension funds, insurance companies, and industrial corporations as holders of Soviet debt instruments. The Soviets apparently believe that this would create new, large avenues of untied Western borrowing and establish influential groups with a vested interest in politically supporting continued and expanded Western economic and financial concessions to the Soviet Union.

The West is already providing inordinate and intrinsically unjustified levels of economic and financial support for Soviet client states, and the USSR, by expanding its presence in the international financial system, intends to promote an increase of these capitalist subventions of Soviet-allied, Marxist economies. Western European and multilateral institutions together have provided approximately $1 billion in outright grants and concessional loans to the Sandinista government of Nicaragua since 1981. The United States Export-Import Bank continues to disburse $50 million to the Marxist government of Angola under existing credit arrangements.

Eastern European nations have worked out similar arrangements with international financial institutions and are seeking to expand them.

Most worrisome of all, the USSR is now attempting to lighten the burden of its economic difficulties, to increase its freedom to maneuver, and to permanently circumvent potential adversaries of its financial dealings by gaining membership in the General Agreement on Tariffs and Trade (GATT), the International Monetary Fund (IMF), the Asian Development Bank (ADB), and other Western institutions. It is interesting to note that the USSR is pursuing this course at the same time it is seeking to undermine these institutions: it has actively supported the Cuban and Nicaraguan campaigns to persuade Latin debtor nations to repudiate their debt obligations to Western banks.

There are a number of steps that the United States should take in concert with Western governments and financial institutions to disengage the USSR from easy access to Western capital. These effort have been best articulated by Roger W. Robinson, from 1982-85, the senior director for international economic affairs of the National Security Council, and currently a Washington consultant. His suggestions include:

1) The recognition that untied Western lending to potential adversaries is unwise from both the commercial perspective and the perspective of national security and that a solution must be multilateral and voluntary in order to be successful. A voluntary approach is likely to garner the widest support, appeal to commercial common sense, and minimize the chance of encumbering only U.S. banks while non-American banks compensate to the benefit of themselves and the Soviet Union.

2) Increased efforts by Western banks to verify the specific uses to which their loans are put by the Eastern Bloc nations, including the Soviet Union. Loans should be tied to capital equipment exports, commodity transactions, or tightly structured and closely scheduled projects. The maturities of these loans should be strictly matched against the duration of the underlying transactions.

3) The closing of egregious gaps in Western statistical reporting, so that both Western analysts and policymakers can more precisely estimate the amount of credits and deposits available to the USSR and its allies. The West, still in a position of international financial dominance and capitalizing upon the relative financial weakness of the Eastern Bloc, can and should demand much more financial disclosure from Eastern Bloc borrowers. In addition, the West could examine more carefully the quality of Soviet loans to other countries. U.S. banks should aggregate their interbank deposit exposure to *all* Soviet-owned entities and periodically report these aggregate exposures to U.S. bank regulators, if they do not already do so. The same practices also should be applied regarding Eastern European banks. The United States should encourage

the banks of other Western nations to adopt these practices, and it should facilitate the gathering, pooling, and dissemination of this information by both banks and governments.

4) Thus, the United States should encourage the Organization for Economic Cooperation and Development (OECD) to establish and endorse a program to monitor Soviet credit activity. Similarly, the OECD should promote Western cooperation with a program to tie all Western loans to the East Bloc to specific projects and terms. Robinson reports that

> there are precedents for such a role by the OECD, including: its action in July, 1982 to eliminate preferential terms on government-backed credits to the USSR; the agreement within the International Energy Agency, under the OECD, to limit Soviet deliveries of natural gas to Western Europe; and more recently, the OECD agreement on tied credits which discourages excess use of grant money in development loans.

5) The passage into law of bills such as those introduced in the 100th Congress by Senator Jake Garn and Senator William Proxmire. The Financial Export Control Bill would give the president authority to block the transfer of money and other financial resources to adversary countries such as the USSR and nations supporting terrorism. Other legislative approaches include the maintenance of the Stevenson Amendment, which limits Soviet access to U.S. government credits, and bills to facilitate greater bank reporting of international loan and interbank activity and to increase the pooling of this vital information.

6) Expanded efforts to limit the Soviet ability to issue debt instruments in Western currencies and in the Western markets. Similarly, the United States should be unambiguous in its opposition to Soviet membership in the IMF, the ADB, the World Bank, and GATT and forcefully reject the idea that admission would have a civilizing effect upon the Kremlin. This appears to be the operant philosophy of Secretary of State George Shultz and West German Foreign Minister Hans-Dietrich Genscher. Robinson told *Human Events* on April 11, 1987, that via these memberships the Soviets

> could eventually have access to a large new pool of untied cash, which is unwise from the standpoint of Western security. Second . . . [the Soviets] obviously do not agree with the institutional mission of the IMF and the World Bank, which is to facilitate greater international economic liberalization. Nor do the Soviets subscribe to the market philosophy underpinning these organizations.

At minimum, there should be a full airing of the implications of the Soviets' involvement in these primary Western financial institutions, including a National Security Decision Directive, instead of the current policy vacuum and possible, private endorsement within the State Department of an East-West financial conference on economic cooperation in Europe.   Policymakers must be vigilant that adequate interagency discussion on such crucial economic security matters should not be preempted by a return of the kind of economic détentism that proved so damaging during the Nixon years.   Ultimately, the United States should recognize that in the financial sphere, an enormous imbalance of power exists between the West and the Eastern Bloc.   In this arena, the correlation of forces weighs heavily in favor of the United States, so we should not hesitate to utilize this advantage to rein in Soviet aggressiveness.   Because continued, large-scale Soviet expansionism is dependent upon financial vitality, the United States should do everything it can to limit the Soviet Union's plan to underwrite that expansion parasitizing the Free World.

The USSR, faced with a growing economic gap between its own internal economic strength and the economic health of the West and between its own economic capabilities and its imperial pretensions, will have to confront four choices:

1) a desperate attempt to seize economic resources and thus unilaterally alter the economic and political correlation of forces;
2) a more energetic effort to parasitize Western financial and technical resources;
3) a scaling back of its aggressive plans; or
4) the serious undertaking of internal economic reform, something that would threaten the power and legitimacy of the *nomenklatura*.

By applying economic pressure now, the United States can assure that the ultimate Soviet decision is that which is the most circumscribed and the one more likely to elicit an effective response from a still economically vital Free World.

A Strategy of Democracy

A strategy designed to counter the Soviet salient should make greater use of America's strengths, such as democracy, freedom, and devotion to human rights.   Free enterprise, especially that practiced by laissez-faire corporate ambassadors of the American system, is inconsistent, unguided, and too often counterproductive to America's interests.   The United States needs a policy that actively promotes, teaches and inculcates democratic values.   This is a dialectic that Marxist-Leninists are at pains to avoid.   Against the appeal of genuine economic, social, and political democracy, the Soviet Union has no defense, even in nations that have had little experience with nonauthoritarian systems of government.

In a sense, the United States has already embarked on such a program, but it requires more resources, more coherence, and more commitment from the government. During the Reagan administration, considerable attention has been paid to restoring democracy in a variety of nations, many of them clients of the United States. In the last decade, particular progress has been made in Central America (Guatemala, El Salvador), South America (Argentina, Peru, Uruguay, Ecuador, Bolivia, and Brazil), and East Asia (the Philippines, the Republic of Korea, and Taiwan). There has also been a more problematical democratizing trend in Africa.

It is clear that the institutions of democracy—open parties, fair and free elections, the right to petition, a system of checks and balances— are effective tools to combat the attraction of authoritarian Marxist-Leninist solutions. Yet they cannot be fully operative unless they are coupled with social and economic democracy, which invariably means land reform, the end to police-state tactics on the local level, and most important of all, the containment and hopefully the elimination of corruption.

The lessons of Fulgencio Batista's Cuba, General Anastasio Somoza's Nicaragua, and the Kuomintang in China should be appreciated for the warnings they represent. The United States cannot accept anticommunism as a tradeoff for corruption and repression in its clients. What a region and the West stand to lose by the malfeasance of one ruling group is so great that deference to local pride and putatively larger considerations of immediate American national interest must not be allowed to determine the political choices the United States must make as the protector of the West.

Today there is an *expectation* among citizens worldwide that the United States is genuinely concerned about injustice and will speak out about it. This expectation is a product of the information revolution. The United States enhances its image and influence when it remains true to these expectations; it damages its credibility and the attraction of the West when it remains silent in the name of superficial realpolitik. The next administration, therefore, should consider an enhanced National Endowment for Democracy, which would facilitate the democratic emergence of many Third World countries. Interestingly, the United States now treads cautiously in this regard, fearing charges of meddling or of putative CIA manipulation. Yet there is a maximum-minimum crossing point: If the United States made the promotion of democracy a much more central part of its policy, then the concerns about profile and the level of involvement would be lessened since the intention of the policy would be unambiguous. One should consider what an unfettered, heavy-handed economic presence the United States maintains worldwide today and use that—and not some ideal of noninvolvement—as the standard by which we would judge an American policy that directly promotes the values and practices of democracy.

The annual financial commitment the United States makes today to such activities is less than the cost of a fighter squadron, yet the potential payoff is immense. Outlays to such institutions as the National Democratic Institute, the National Republican Institute, and the foreign training institutes of the AFL-CIO and the Chamber of Commerce should be expanded. These institutions and others have already developed a wide curriculum of programs that actually *build democracy* on both the local and national levels. They have been at pains to involve indigenous partners and utilize local expertise. The USSR, through its various Marxist institutes, is redoubling its efforts in this direction, but it can only compete with the U.S. model in a situation of endemic local oppression and where the United States chooses not to act.

There should be a radical enlargement of the present efforts to promote understanding of Western policy among all the peoples and nations of the world, as well as to counter the formidable Soviet programs of disinformation and misinformation that are causing so much damage to the U.S. image throughout the world. Among these methods, it could be useful to hold Soviet spokesmen accountable to Western opinion through open sessions like those within the Helsinki format. Also, more resources should be devoted to making the American case, through radio, television, and the direct satellite broadcasts so feared by the Soviets. The United States should make discussions of the true nature of Russian and Soviet society, Soviet and Russian goals and methods, psychology, and so forth. High-priority items in a world already tuned in to the American electronic and cultural message.

A Strategy for Human Rights

The United States must confront Soviet moral thuggery. The natural complement to a U.S. strategy to promote democracy is a strategy to promote human rights. The only course that corresponds to the interests and ideals of Western civilization is to make the achievement of genuine peace with freedom the compass and lodestar of Western policy. The United States and its allies have more than enough potential power to achieve that goal through the methods of alliance diplomacy and in peace. It will take effort and time to do so, and it will not be easy or cheap, but it must be done. We have retreated for too long, and the cause of freedom can scarcely afford any future defeats.

The championing of human rights is one of the strongest advantages the United States possesses against the Soviet Union. Here, too, however, as with the appeal of democracy, the United States has not made full use of the strengths and tools at its disposal, nor has it exploited the extreme Soviet weakness both internally and internationally in this regard. During the first two years of the Carter administration, for example, the United States made considerable capital out of Soviet shortcomings in the field of human rights. Yet when the USSR made the expected response, a threatening and defensive assertion of control over its own internal affairs, the Carter administration (typically) retreated.

For the last two years of his presidency, Jimmy Carter focused the moral ardor of the United States on U.S. allies exclusively, some of whom, like the shah of Iran, were destabilized as a result. Throughout the world, nations and individuals were disconcerted and confused by a fainthearted and unjustified American retreat from a program that had captured the imagination of the world. Like so many other actions of the discredited Carter administration, this action sowed cynicism about the United States that still damages our image and vitiates our influence.

The USSR gave the West a powerful and as yet barely utilized tool over its behavior in the Basket Three section of the Helsinki Accords. Basket Three provides both definitions and the means by which signatories have the right to raise the issue of human rights abuses. In the face of Basket Three's potentially embarrassing provisions, the Kremlin has chosen to ignore, repress, or circumvent those in and outside the country who would bring the USSR to account. It has retreated into its predictable (and under Basket Three, unjustified) citation of sovereignty over its internal affairs. But a renewed, vigorous, undeterred pursuit of Soviet human rights violations by the Western allies, acting under the Basket Three provisions, would have a profoundly unsettling effect upon the USSR both internally and abroad.

Internally, it would accelerate the contradictions that have already been sparked by Gorbachev's endorsement of *glasnost* and simultaneous hard line on true democratization and devolution of power from the *nomenklatura*. Externally, it would discredit the USSR's arrogant and Orwellian counterstrategy of endorsing Marxist economic "human rights." The representatives of Soviet adventurism would find that the Soviet system and its overall message had become an issue and not "international imperialism" exclusively, as has been the case heretofore. Specific American successes in promoting the restoration of human rights will only push the entire process along even faster. Simply raising the world's consciousness of the issue markedly enhanced America's standing and influence in 1977.

In the case of human rights, as with the cause of democracy, much of the world—including most of the citizens of the Eastern Bloc and the

People's Republic of China—*expect* the United States to take the lead and set an example. People throughout the world understand what the United States means by "human rights"; the effect of the Western electronic culture has amplified the natural human predisposition to freedom from oppression. Thus, reticence by the United States on this subject should *not* be excused as a reflection of sophisticated diplomacy or a concession to realpolitik. On the contrary, a sophisticated diplomatic strategy that conforms to the reality of world politics today will make the pursuit of our standard of human rights in the Soviet Union, among Soviet clients, *and* throughout the world the centerpiece of American foreign policy.

A Strategy for Engagement

Finally, the United States and the West must put themselves on an operational and psychological footing to challenge the Soviet plan for world domination. For Americans used to solutions based on attention to mutual interests and the establishment of genuine trust, this may prove the most difficult step of all. It is already apparent that the USSR is moving to discredit what it apparently sees as a waning anti-Soviet movement in the United States. During the summit in Washington in December 1987, for instance, the head of the Soviet Institute on the United States and Canada, Georgi Arbatov, openly asserted that Gorbachev's goal was to "deprive America of The Enemy."

The Kremlin obviously believes that by lowering egregious areas of conflict and by establishing a moral equivalence between the superpowers it can acquire greater diplomatic room to maneuver internationally while neutralizing reflexive and minority voices of anti-Soviet criticism within the United States. Unquestionably, if the United States moves institutionally in the directions outlined above, the Soviets will try early on to persuade Congress and the media that an American counterstrategy against the USSR is both warlike and unnecessary. The Soviets appreciate Sun Tzu's dictum about the desirability of defeating the enemy's strategy; they are certainly not above trying to strangle it in its crib.

Education

Thus, policymakers must appreciate that the first task of a strategy of engagement is education. They must be prepared to make the case for an overall strategy to contain the USSR and for the energetic, unrelenting prosecution of that strategy. At first by their very existence and then by their successful operations, a national strategy office and an aggregate threat assessment office will provide policymakers with the information and rationales for a sustained strategy. By disengaging itself from arms control diplomacy, the United States can minimize the political attraction of peace "spectaculars" with the USSR that have the effect of paralyzing or suspending U.S. actions against Soviet adventurism while facilitating further Soviet military and political gains.

Pipes has characterized the Soviet economy as a war economy operating at moderate efficiency. This is also true of Soviet foreign and internal policies. In both instances, there are clear aspects of a war mentality. Although at times the subversion of U.S. interests throughout the world may be pursued with a measure of restraint and the depiction of the United States in the Soviet media does not equal that afforded the Nazis, this does not mean that the essential character of the Soviet approach to the West is not warlike. The managers of American policy must be prepared to make this point and document it. The evidence is readily available, and more important, the American people are smart enough to assimilate it, a fact politicians frequently forget.

The Burden of Proof

The second task of a strategy of engagement is the development of countertactics that put the onus on one's opponent. When the Soviets move to discredit an energetic American counterstrategy, the reflexive American response must be a demand for modifications in the Soviet Union sufficient to convince us (and an objective world opinion) that the USSR is, in fact, not on a war footing. Thus, by implementing both the means and plans of a counterstrategy, the United States can better position itself to defend its case for that strategy and make Soviet behavior assume the burden of making that defense. It then will be able to promote its solution, or reforms in Soviet political, economic, and diplomatic behavior. And in the face of the almost certain inevitable Soviet rejection of this, the case for the American counterstrategy and its continued implementation will have been demonstrated by the USSR's own actions.

On the off chance that the Soviet leadership shows some willingness to make some modifications (for internal or external political or economic reasons), the United States certainly will not be hurt by this de-escalation. Indeed, a working strategy would offer the Soviet leadership blandishments to move in this direction. (The national strategy office, integrating the opinions of the CIA, the Commerce Department, and State Department, could develop a list of suggestions.) Such blandishments might succeed; at minimum, they would show the United States to be responsive and flexible; and they are certain to cause discord in the Soviet ruling group. But these proffered compensations must be tied to specific Soviet performance, and more important, they must not include a dismantling of America's own counterstrategy. A national strategy office would prepare policymakers to anticipate and deflect a Soviet countermove in this direction.

This sort of approach can and should be employed in a thousand different engagements, large and small. The Soviets already use it constantly with us. The subsequent American and Western responses—to negotiate among ourselves, to assume the onus for accommodation, to rationalize the Soviet position—are profoundly self-destructive, which the Soviets deliberately try to promote. A shifting of the responsibility back to the Soviet leadership is the best response. The United States can accomplish this with good tactics, preparedness, tenacity, a sense of public relations, and a clear sense of larger strategic objectives. By using the newly installed strategy institutions to educate both the American public and Washington about the realities of long-term strategy, the United States ultimately may foster a *cultural* change, such that people come to naturally distrust the sort of superficial, short-term political gains and vacant hopes for a new era of peace that accompany arms control and summit diplomacy.

Fostering Values

This aspect of cultural change points up the need to inculcate values and attitudes among the public and especially among the strategists and managers of policy themselves. This is different from the first task described above, or the need for empirical education about the reality of the Soviet threat and the justification of an American strategy to meet it. In some ways, the inculcation of values and attitudes is more important for without a set of values, policymakers cannot have any real sense of vision or judgment or understanding. Lacking values, policymakers cannot establish priorities, distinguish among possible tactics, or know when to accept sacrifices and when to be obdurate. Certainly, Soviet strategists and policymakers have a clear sense of values involving a combination of Marxist imperatives to revolution, Leninist imperatives to rule, and bureaucratic imperatives to survive. For Americans, values and attitudes should include an appreciation of the following:

- that the objective of the entire enterprise is not some ephemeral bureaucratic or political gain but the cause of freedom and the vanquishing of a mechanistic, inhumane tyranny;
- that the United States is engaged in an ongoing battle, in which clear-cut victories may be difficult to achieve and in which the adversary is unlikely to concede anything, no matter how obvious

the defeat appears to be or how much time has passed;
- that small victories should be valued;
- that victories must be sustained once they are achieved;
- that there is a utility in having limited objectives;
- that these objectives must be fully defined;
- that limited resources must be husbanded and advantages utilized freely and fully;
- that countermoves and likely targets must be constantly adduced and evaluated;
- that one must allow for the unexpected and the irrational and be prepared to identify opportunities, decline them intelligently, or seize them;
- that potential and unexpected allies must be identified and supported;
- that initiatives and tactics should be integrated and mutually reinforcing;
- that the essential responsibility of the policymaker is to guard against hubris and gamesmanship for its own sake; and
- that one must develop a strategy for effectively *implementing* strategy.

Taking Risks

This appreciation of established values leads to the fourth and final task of a strategy for engagement: to engage. Strategists must appreciate that the Soviet threat does not rest. Yet like Heraclitus's river, it is forever evolving. Thus, it cannot be perfectly defined or perfectly met. Policymakers, strategists, and the American people must appreciate that a counterstrategy is a human endeavor and thus a percentage deal. Flawless stratagems are the province of fiction, and the fact that some approaches do not succeed fully and even fail at times should not deter the United States from its larger responsibility.

Preparing for setbacks is perhaps the most important part of the strategic process. Without this ability, strategic endeavor grinds to a halt. In many ways, past administrations have not prepared for setbacks, and the fitful disarray of American policy is the result. By having a mechanism to assess the threat and develop strategy and by cultivating an attitude that values and appreciates strategy, the United States can increase the chances of success and minimize the evolution of tactical and strategic, short-term and long-term failures.

Our imperative must be to engage and to try, not to wait and hope. This does not mean that blind enthusiasm and good intentions are sufficient, but we should avoid the millennialist, Spenglerian denigration of that singular American characteristic, the belief in our power to accomplish things. The United States did not become the leader in the cause of freedom by doubting the essential rightness of its cause or by rejecting every success as imperfect.

Simply by engaging the Soviets *intelligently* and with foresight, the United States can impede and complicate Soviet designs. Simply by evincing a reasoned—not merely reflexive—consistency and resolve, the United States can force the Soviet leadership to question its own confidence and its own strategies. By challenging the Soviet definition of the conflict and utilizing our democratic strengths to buttress our case, the United States can embolden potential proponents of freedom and dishearten totalitarians. By confronting the Soviet threat on the same scale that it confronts us, we can impose limitations and a sense of our reality upon the Kremlin.

Over time, the Soviet leadership will come to see itself not as the avant-garde of historical inevitability but as the harried protectors of a crumbling domain. Soviet "Grand Strategy" abroad will come to resemble Soviet reality at home: bullying and intermittently violent to be sure, but inherently divided, fearful, conservative, and inadequate to meet the needs of the modern world.

By utilizing the strategic approaches described herein, by building consensus, and by being mindful of the need for a coherent strategy to advance Western interests and confront Soviet designs, the United States can halt the seemingly inexorable spread of the Soviet empire. With patience, luck, and tenacity, we may initiate an historic reversal. Over time, the reward for our efforts may become apparent to every citizen of the world.

Index